LUTHER
AND
PRAYER

LUTHER AND PRAYER

Martin E. Lehmann

NORTHWESTERN PUBLISHING HOUSE
Milwaukee, Wisconsin

Library of Congress Card 85-61238
Northwestern Publishing House
1250 N. 113th St., P.O. Box 26975, Milwaukee, WI 53226-0975
© 1985 by Northwestern Publishing House. All rights reserved
Published 1985
Printed in the United States of America
ISBN 0-8100-0216-7

CONTENTS

PART THREE
Prayer As Fruit of the Spirit's Work

INTRODUCTION

Prayer is a phenomenon common to all religions in the world. Whether it be in primitive religions or in the more developed religions of advanced cultures, prayer plays a fundamental role in all of them.

> For what are men better than sheep or goats
> That nourish a blind life within the brain,
> If, knowing God, they lift not hands of
>   prayer
> Both for themselves and those who call
>   them friend?[1]

This rhetorical question from Alfred Tennyson's poem "Morte D'Arthur" fittingly underlines the imperative of human prayer. Friedrich Heiler in his epoch-making book *Prayer* calls prayer "the central phenomenon of religion," and goes so far as to state that "prayer is the great bond of union of Christendom and not only of all Christendom, but of all mankind."[2] Heiler carefully traces the development and history of prayer in the religions of the world and shows how prayer was first uttered by individuals and groups. He asserts, "The free spontaneous petitionary prayer of the natural man exhibits the prototype of all prayer."[3]

On the basis of his investigation of prayer life in the context of the many religions of humankind,

Heiler proposed the generally valid and accepted distinction between two main types of prayer, the mystical and the prophetic. He describes the mystical prayer as contemplative, striving to achieve the union of the individual with God, while the prophetic prayer, presupposing God's revelation of himself, is found to be emotional, as it addresses God personally and seeks his direction and help in life. Prophetic prayer is therefore dialogical in its basic structure.

In the Hebrew-Christian tradition prayer is preeminently prophetic because the concept of revelation is the controlling factor in its religious development. In all the books of the Bible as the record of God's self-revelation this prophetic type of prayer prevails and exercises a very important function. God's personal address through his self-disclosure in Scripture has the explicit purpose of calling forth the believing response of a person or persons hearing it. On the basis of the relationship of faith thus established, prayer becomes both possible and necessary. The Book of Psalms or the Psalter, for example, consists almost entirely of prayers, petitions, and praises to God and of exhortations to live a godly life of thanksgiving and trust in him. In addition to this, prophetic prayers, uttered by men and women of faith among the many vicissitudes of life, abound throughout the Scriptures. And in the last book of the Bible, the Revelation of John, there is a picturesque reference to "golden bowls full of incense" which symbolize "the prayers of the saints" that rise unceasingly up to God (Revelation 5:8).

The history of the church of Jesus Christ from apostolic times to the present bears witness to the unbroken continuity of the prayers that have been offered to God by his people. Indeed, a believing church is a praying church, even as a true Christian is a praying Christian. The more vital the faith of the people of God the more fervent and forceful are the prayers that are brought to him.

The early and the medieval church furnish us with many examples of a magnificently intense prayer life. One could without difficulty compile a long list of such persons from these bygone centuries of church history whose Christian witness and prayers were conspicuously notable and inspiring. In the early church there were — to mention but a few — Ignatius of Antioch, Athanasius, Basil of Caesarea, Irenaeus, Cyprian, Ambrose, Monica and her son Augustine. In the Middle Ages names like St. Martin of Tours, Boniface, Bernard of Clairvaux, Anselm of Canterbury, Francis of Assisi, Thomas Aquinas, Catherine of Siena and Mechthild of Magdeburg deserve to be mentioned.

In the age of the Reformation, too, prayer came to have renewed and profound significance in the church in spite of the tragic divisions which occurred at that time in the Western Church. It was a time when Christian piety expressed itself in many different forms. There are numerous leaders of reform and renewal during this historical period who merit scrutiny and study with respect to their spirituality, their emphasis on prayer, and their understanding and practice of it. Among them Martin Luther has been singled out in this study as the one whose recovery of the central message of Scripture, the gospel of God's redeeming love in Christ, enabled him to speak authoritatively and engagingly on matters of faith and prayer. His profound insights into the nature of the Christian faith are of pivotal importance, and their impact on Christianity is felt to this day.

Martin Luther (1483-1546) was the earliest among the reformers of the sixteenth century. He still stands before us as a spiritual giant and makes it possible for us to explore his theology of prayer and the meaning it had for him and believers of his day on the basis of his writings and his activities in and for the church. It is clear that his understanding of prayer can in no way be isolated from the totality of his theology. Indeed, it can be said that prayer is an integral and significant part of his entire theology.

PART ONE
PRAYER AS GOD'S DESIGN

CHAPTER ONE

THE NEED FOR PRAYER

Luther as a monk in the cloister at Erfurt fell heir to the discipline, worship, study, self-mortification and prayer as these were practiced in all their rigor according to the prescriptions of the strict Observantine branch of the Augustinian Order. Probably even before he was received as a member of the Order he was given a personal copy of the Bible "with the red leather binding," the Vulgate, which he was "industriously to read, thoughtfully to hear, and carefully to study."[1] It was in connection with his wrestling with the message and meaning of the Scriptures in the monastery and later as a lecturer on the Bible that he came to a fuller and deeper comprehension of faith and prayer in the church and in his own personal life against the background of their more traditional connotation.

A GROWING UNDERSTANDING OF THE NEED FOR PRAYER

In his First Lectures on the Psalms Luther evidences his concern for prayer, designating "especially earnest prayer" as "the ascent of the mind to God."[2] Luther contrasts ancient times, "when there was juice and blood in the church" and "out of a rich anointing there were joyful praises of God," with the prevailing situation in which prayers are offered "in a hoarse and laborious way."[3] In commenting on Psalm 70, he states that the Psalm "is to be commended to all priests, so that they will not mumble it coldly and perfunctorily, but help the church of God with this prayer with all their heart."[4] He also encourages believers to ask "great and many things" from God in prayer. At the same time he cautions against restricting prayer narrowly to oneself alone; "but prayer should be made for all that is good and for all men."[5]

In his opening comments on Psalm 102 Luther observes that no one can recite it in prayer "except one who is poor in spirit and has begun to loathe the vanity of the world and the goods of the flesh and to long for spiritual blessings." He also holds that a person should pray "not only in the spirit but also with the mind." "The intellect makes the prayer, but the feeling makes the cry, for the latter desires, but the former shows what it should desire, and how and whence, etc."[6] Increasingly Luther is beginning to see prayer in the believer's life as a response to God's word of promise and not as a claim based on one's personal merit. He enlarges on the prayer to God in Psalm 119 in these words: "You have promised Christ and His grace. Therefore I indeed come early before the grace is given and set forth, but no matter how unworthy I am, You are truthful, who made the promise. Nor do I come early and cry because You are my debtor, or because I have earned or am worthy of so great a reward. . . , but because I hoped in Your words."[7]

After his early lectures on the Psalms, from 1513 to 1515, Luther came to grasp the biblical teaching on prayer with greater clarity. From 1515-1516 he expounded on St. Paul's Letter to the Romans. The admonition, "Be constant in prayer" (Romans 12:12), induced Luther to rebuke those who simply read the Psalms in a perfunctory manner without putting their heart into it. In the first place, God is thus offended all the more in accordance with the prophetic word, "This people honors me with their lips, but their heart is far from me" (Matthew 15:8; Isaiah 29:13). Secondly, the thoughtless recital of the prayers contained in the Psalms leads to self-deceit and a sense of security and satisfaction with appearances, as though the prayers had been properly said. The way to genuine prayer is thus blocked; no further efforts to pray with heart-felt sincerity are made; and those who pray in such a way consume the contributions of the people at leisure without a feeling of guilt or negligence.

However, the word "constant" deserves to be heeded especially by the clergy, according to Luther. It is intended to elicit genuine effort, "for as the ancient fathers have said: 'There is no labor so hard as prayer.' " "Therefore when a man wants to enter the priesthood, he must first consider that he is entering a work which is harder than any other, namely, the work of prayer. For this requires a subdued and broken mind and an elevated and victorious spirit."[8]

"Prayer," according to Luther, "is of two kinds." First, there is the outward, spoken prayer (*oratio vocalis*) for which "a virtual intention" is sufficient "as a nice little cover for laziness and negligence," because one can then be satisfied with one's praying without any further effort. But paying attention only to the words, "as monks and others, such as simple lay people do," "is not prayer in the proper sense of the word."[9] Here Luther is still willing to concede that praying in this way constitutes an act of obedience which is pleasing to God and is consequently not to be despised, for it drives away the devil and brings the Holy Spirit to us. This kind of praying is beneficial also "because the divine Word by nature affects the soul, even if it is not understood."[10] In addition to this, intellect and emotion are somehow affected, and, lastly, though persons praying thus do not benefit from the emotional impact of the words, their spirits are nevertheless lifted up to God.

Second, there is the mental, or interior, kind of praying, (oratio mentalis) which is the prayer of the heart. It is incumbent upon the better educated and intelligent to pray in this way by paying attention to the sense and the meaning of the words. Accommodating oneself to what the words that are prayed express, one engages in true prayer. The definition of prayer which Luther then puts forward is the one commonly used in the Middle Ages and derived from John of Damascus, the great teacher of the faith in the Eastern Church. "Mental prayer is the ascent of the mind, or rather of the spirit to God."[11]

This "interior" way of praying is what the Apostle Paul has in mind when he exhorts us to be constant in prayer. Prayer ought to be engaged in frequently and diligently. Luther believes that there is "no other work that requires more labor and effort and therefore is more efficacious and fruitful."[12] The words of Jesus, "the kingdom of heaven has suffered violence, and men of violence take it by force" (Matthew 11:12) refer to the power of prayer. "For prayer in my opinion is a constant violent action of the spirit as it is lifted up to God, as a ship is driven upward against the power of the storm."[13] Through the dynamic force of prayer the kingdom of God, which Christ has inaugurated on earth, is operative among believers. After that violence decreases and disappears, as the Spirit draws and carries the heart upward by grace. Two factors, the deeply felt anxiety of the heart and the drawing, uplifting power of the Spirit, make the impact of prayer tremendous. In fact Luther asserts that "true prayer is omnipotent, as our Lord says: 'For everyone who asks receives, etc.' (Matthew 7:8)."[14] The practice of prayer means therefore engaging in an interior action of force by which one fights against the devil and the flesh.

With regard to the canonical hours for prayer, the church requires merely that the words be spoken; but it cannot prescribe intellectual or emotional attentiveness, since it does not possess the power to demand such inner personal involvement in prayer. For this reason Luther castigates the practice of establishing endowments for canonical hours in the belief that those who make these endowments have it in their power to buy prayer. It would be much better, he says, if persons making such endowments would attach to them no directives and so permit the person who is asked to pray for them to do so when he

7

is in the position to do it. To be sure, foundations of this nature were specifically endowed for the salvation of souls and for the glory of God. But what if such endowments are made in order to boast before others or in a deceitful way and not for the glory of God? It is clear that Luther's prophetic view of prayer is asserting itself with vigor and forthrightness as he hopes that he will prove to be a false prophet when he expresses the fear that the monastery to which he belongs may yet bring great misfortune upon its founder and patron, Elector Frederick the Wise, as well as upon the Church of All Saints.[15]

In these early lectures on the Psalms and on Romans one can observe that Luther is seeking to interpret prayer in a manner that is consonant with the biblical message. His emerging view of prayer causes him to find little value in the outward requirements and in the formal definitions that have a mystical connotation. In fact he is concerned mainly about coming to grips with the true meaning of prayer as a spiritual expression of faith. To be sure, there is as yet no express repudiation of the scholastic definitions of prayer. However, his uneasiness with certain prevailing teachings on it in the church is beginning to surface in his writings. It is also noteworthy that at this early stage of his theological development Luther treasures the Lord's Prayer above all other prayers. His deep appreciation for its content and meaning is evident from his exposition of it and his many comments on it.[16]

By 1520 Luther had decisively rejected the mystical, nonbiblical elements in the church's teaching on prayer. He therefore denounced the writings of Dionysius, the Areopagite, (ca. 500) in his treatise, *The Babylonian Captivity of the Church*. Referring to Dionysius' Neoplatonic writing *Of the Ecclesiastical Hierarchy*, Luther warns against lending credence to its assertions and exhorts his readers to pay attention to the scriptural witness. "But in his Theology," he points out "which is rightly called *Mystical*, of which certain ignorant theologians make so much, he is downright dangerous, for he is more of a Platonist than a Christian." Indeed, if Luther could have his way, he would have believers disregard his books because through them they do not learn about Jesus Christ but rather tend to forget what they already know of him. "Let us rather hear Paul, that we may learn Jesus Christ and him crucified (1 Corinthians 2:2). He is the way, the life, and the truth; he is the ladder (Genesis 28:12) by which we come to the Father, as he says: 'No one comes to the Father, but by me' (John 14:6)."[17]

With this growing concentration on the biblical testimony Luther gave proof that his prophetic view of prayer, based on scriptural sources, would dominate almost entirely whatever he would have to say and teach on prayer and thus what he would also put into practice in his own life and the Christian community. From 1518 onward, then, it can be surmised that his understanding of prayer in its meaning and purpose was determined in a decisive way by the biblical witness and its explicit directives. In this light he developed and set forth his theology of prayer in his career as a teacher and preacher in the church.

9

GOD'S WORD AND FAITH
AS PREREQUISITES FOR PRAYER

When God's Word calls forth faith it will result in prayer in that person's life. "Christendom, and every Christian soul, is born in and through the Word of God."[18] Without this Word of God both trust in God and our prayer to him are not possible. It is therefore incumbent upon the spiritual leaders of the church to make known the Word of God continuously and abundantly. Only the Word can nourish, preserve and protect persons in their life of faith in God. Moreover, we have the assurance that "God never permits his Word to go forth without leading to fruit. He himself is present and teaches inwardly that which he gives externally through the priest. In Isaiah 55[:10-11] he says, 'For as the rain waters the earth and makes it fruitful, so shall my word be that goes forth from my mouth; it shall not return to me empty, but it shall accomplish that for which I sent it.' This is what creates true Christians, who know Christ and who deeply savor him."[19]

Through the Word of God we become children of God. And since that Word first addressed us in baptism, we have in this way become God's own people.[20] God became our Father so that "the name of God, in which we were baptized, works all this in us. But we should always pray that the name of God may abide in us, be active in us, and be hallowed."[21] Here Luther equates the name of God with the Word of God, ascribing to it the power by which we are made God's children who through our rebirth in baptism by means of the Word have the privilege and obligation to pray. A right relationship to God is thus established in us by the power of the Word as it addresses us in our lostness and need.

The God who speaks to us in his Word is the revealed God (*deus revelatus*). In his exposition of Psalm 51 Luther warns explicitly against each and every attempt to seek to know God apart from his Word and promises. Outside of the revelation of his Word we are confronted by "the absolute God," or "the naked God" (*deus nudus*). Whenever we try to rise to God in our speculations and think of him as he is in himself we risk self-destruction. The revelation of God in Scripture is designed to keep us from pursuing such a dangerous and death-dealing path. For that reason Luther notes that "David is talking with the God of his fathers, with the God who promised." When we search for God in his Word and let him deal with us through the mask of his Word we are on the right track. David, Luther reminds us, "is speaking with God as He is dressed and clothed in His Word and promises, so that from the name 'God' we cannot exclude Christ, whom God promised to Adam and other patriarchs. We must take hold of this God, not naked but clothed and revealed in His Word; otherwise certain despair will crush us."

There is a distinction to be made between the prophets, who speak with God on the basis of his revelation, and the Gentiles, who have no such revelation. The latter speak with God apart from his Word according to their own thoughts; but the biblical writers speak with God in accordance with his self-revelation which he has clothed in his Word and

11

promises. "This God, clothed in such a kind appearance and, so to speak, in such a pleasant mask, that is to say, dressed in His promises — this God we can grasp and look at with joy and trust."[22] Such a revelation of God through his Word becomes the basis for true trust in God in the lives of persons, making it possible, yes, necessary for them to speak to God in prayer. All other ways and means to establish a relationship with God are foredoomed to failure because outside of his Word there is futile speculation about the nature and purpose of God so that one must ultimately despair of achieving one's goal of coming to God. In the midst of uncertainty, scepticism and doubt the Word conveys the sure and certain message of God's fatherly forgiveness and love for us. God comes to us in our need, through his Word. He reestablishes a new relationship of trust in him and obedience to his will by that same Word, renewing and strengthening our faith daily. In our prayers we express our trust in him and our dependence on him on the basis of this person-to-person relationship which by his free initiative and the mighty creative power of his Word of love he has established for us and in us.

The proper sequence for prayer is indicated in the way in which God's revelation of himself comes to us. We are first confronted by the Ten Commandments with their stern demands. In that light we come to recognize our sickness-unto-death, our sin and need. Then the Apostles' Creed points us to God and his forgiving and restoring mercy in Christ which, by the Spirit's working in us, we embrace in faith. Finally, the Lord's Prayer teaches us to pray for the full realization of our new, God-given status as children of God and disciples of Jesus Christ. "In these three," concludes Luther, "are the essentials of the Bible."[23] Thus prayer possesses a determinative function in the life and history of the people of God on earth.

In his Large Catechism Luther describes our human predicament and God's prescriptive solution to the problem. Our situation is such that we cannot keep the Ten Commandments perfectly, although we have come to faith in Christ. The forces of evil, the devil, the world and our own flesh, deter us in doing God's will. "Consequently nothing is so necessary as to call upon God incessantly and to drum into his ears our prayer that he may give, preserve and increase in us faith and obedience to the Ten Commandments and remove all that stands in our way and hinders us from fulfilling them. That we may know what and how to pray, our Lord Christ himself has taught us both the way and the words. . . ."[24]

Faith is always the correlate of the Word of God. The Word is proclaimed to awaken faith, and prayer is the activity of faith. "Prayer is nothing else than the lifting up of heart or mind to God. But if the lifting up of the heart constitutes the essence and nature of prayer, it follows that everything else which does not invite the lifting up of the heart is not prayer."[25] In the light of this definition of prayer Luther can speak of "spiritual prayer, which may be carried on without interruption, even during physical labors."[26] However, the perfect accomplishment of spiritual prayer presupposes a constant and strong faith which no one possesses. Nevertheless, faith must be exercised in prayer and grow thereby.[27]

Contrariwise, prayer is acceptable only when it "breathes a firm confidence and trust that it will be heard (no matter how small and unworthy it may be in itself) because of the reliable pledge and promise of God. Not your zeal but God's Word and promise render your prayer good. This faith, based on God's Word, is also the true worship; without it all other worship is sheer deception and error."[28] From this it is apparent how faith and prayer are intimately bound together. Prayer always proceeds on the basis of faith in God's word of promise.

Luther distinguishes clearly between two kinds of faith. First, faith may mean simply the acceptance of what is said about God as "an item of knowledge." But this is not true faith. The true believer puts his trust in God and acts on his conviction that what has been promised by God in his Word is altogether sure. "Only a faith that ventures everything in life and in death on what is said [in Scripture] of God makes a person a Christian and obtains all he desires from God. No corrupt or hypocritical heart can have such a faith; this is a living faith as the First Commandment demands: I am your God; you shall have no other gods."[29] This kind of faith alone is the true faith, and it "is given only by God himself." The paradoxical nature of faith is thus set forth. It is a divine gift; but it is at the same time the individual's vital and personal response to God's word of promise by reason of which a person declares, "I believe."

14

The constant temptation exists to pray selfishly in faith, to seek our own advantage in prayer, and to forget others. The opening words of the Lord's Prayer, "Our Father," however, remind us that together we might say "our Father" and not "my Father." Laying aside all hatred, envy and discord, we should love each other as God's children and pray for all persons.[30] When our prayers are said with genuine trust toward God in our hearts, doubts will be dispelled and neither a No nor a Maybe can mar the certainty of God's Yes to our supplications.[31] In the light of the need for true trust in God as a prerequisite for praying, Luther could make the observation that "praying is a rare work, which no one does but Christians. At the same time it was very common in the world."[32] Without trust in God there can be no real prayer. Yet precisely because faith is God's gift to his people, it is "the particular work of Christians, who have the Spirit of God, not to be lax and lazy, but incessant and constant in their praying...."[33] Whenever faith is lacking, prayer becomes a sham and pretense, "mere jabbering and babbling," and not the experience of the heart. God is not concerned about the number of our prayers nor with their length, but about their genuineness, as they proceed from the heart in faith.

In his exposition of Psalm 90 Luther calls upon his hearers to be guided by Moses, who, "in true faith of the heart, prays and says: 'Thou art our Dwelling Place.' " Such a prayer cannot be spoken from the heart "without faith and without the gift of the Holy Spirit" because faith is essential in true prayer.[34]

Faith and prayer cannot be separated. Faith, based on the Word of God, is a confident trust in God's grace, goodness and forgiveness, and issues in prayers that are heard by God at all times and in all places. "If we conclude our prayer with the word 'Amen' spoken with confidence and strong faith, it is surely sealed and heard."[35]

Because faith is the prerequisite for true prayer a mere recital of the words of a prayer is of no benefit or blessing if the heart is not in it. Luther is of the opinion that too much reliance is placed on prayers that are simply recited and esteemed more highly than the Lord's Prayer. "It would be better to pray one Lord's Prayer," advises Luther, "with a devout heart and with thought given to the words, resulting in a better life, than for you to acquire absolution through reciting all other prayers."[36] Some persons, claims Luther, fail to derive the desired spiritual strength and blessing from their prayer. "They nullify it, for they utter it merely with their lips and not with their hearts, because they will not believe that they are heard until they know, or imagine that they know, that they have prayed well and worthily. Thus they build on themselves."[37] The lack of faith coupled with a false reliance on what such persons have and do by themselves makes their prayer meaningless and empty verbiage. "What is important for a good prayer," says Luther in his *Personal Prayer Book* of 1522, "is not many words, . . . but rather a turning to God frequently and with heartfelt longing, and doing so without ceasing."[38]

Luther's commentary on Matthew 6:7, "And in

praying do not heap up empty phrases as the Gentiles do; for they think that they will be heard for their many words," deals at length with the futility of engaging in long prayers which he calls "a reckless and worthless prattle, the sort of thing that would come from people who supposed that they would not be heard otherwise."[39] He believes that the inhabitants of monasteries and cloisters as well as the clergy in general have become wrongly obsessed with the necessity of wearing themselves out by spending much time in prayer and by singing and reading their canonical hours at night. They are suffering from "the gentile delusion" that the more praying they do "the holier and greater an act of worship" would seem to be. In reality, however, their prayers are "the slave labor of their mouths or their tongues."

But true prayer, as Jesus himself explained, is the language of faith and comes from the heart. "For God does not ask how much or how long you have prayed, but how good the prayer is and whether it proceeds from the heart."[40] Therefore trust in God's grace is the *sine qua non* of all praying.

GOD'S COMMAND TO PRAY

Time and again Luther focuses on God's explicit command that believers should pray. For that reason prayer "may be prompted by sheer obedience."[41] Not only the promise of God to hear us but also his command that we pray is therefore an important reason for praying.[42]

In his *Personal Prayer Book* Luther comments on

17

the opening words of the Lord's Prayer, "Our Father who art in heaven," by the formulation of a prayer to God. "O Almighty God," he begins, "in your unmerited goodness to us and through the merit and mediation of your only beloved Son, Jesus Christ, you have permitted and even commanded and taught us to regard you and call upon you as one Father of us all."[43] Besides, we should do what Christ commands us to do as his disciples. "Pray for those who spitefully abuse you and persecute you," said Jesus. "Then it is our duty to pray and to commend our cause to God, for on earth we have no law or judge to vindicate us."[44]

Nowhere does Luther make the divine mandate to pray more explicit in his writings than in his two Catechisms. "Prayer," he reminds us in his Large Catechism, "therefore, is as strictly and solemnly commanded as all the other commandments, such as having no other God, not killing, not stealing, etc."[45] To disregard this clear command to pray by expressing personal doubt about the need and helpfulness of prayer and by excusing oneself on the assumption that someone else will engage in prayer if one neglects to pray is wrong. Such thoughts and actions cause a person to fall into the habit of not praying at all. But simply babbling or bellowing prayers is not true prayer either, even if it is done in church. "To pray, as the Second Commandment teaches, is to call upon God in every need. This God requires of us; he has not left it to our choice. It is our duty and obligation to pray if we want to be Christians, just as it is our duty to obey our fathers and our mothers and the civil authorities."[46]

18

In the light of the fact that prayer is clearly commanded we should face the inescapable truth that we have no right to despise prayer, but should value it highly. Luther compares obedience to the command to pray with the obedience of a child to his father and mother. A child, reflecting on the commandment to obey his parents, will do so because God has given the commandment and out of reverence for God will obey it. "So, too, here," infers Luther. "What we shall pray, and for what, we should regard as demanded by God and done in obedience to him. We should think 'On my account this prayer would amount to nothing; but it is important because God has commanded it.' So, no matter what he has to pray for, everybody should always approach God in obedience to this commandment."[47]

In his explanation of the Second Commandment in the Small Catechism, Luther likewise sees the command to pray to God embedded in the prohibition not to use the name of God in vain. Accordingly "we should not use his name to curse, swear, practice magic, lie or deceive, but in every time of need call upon him, pray to him, and give him thanks."[48] Summing up the whole of the Lord's Prayer in his comment on the meaning of the Amen spoken at the conclusion, he observes that the prayer should be said in the assurance that its petitions are acceptable to and heard by the heavenly Father, "for he himself commanded us to pray like this and promised to hear us."[49]

In his sermons, too, Luther impressed upon his congregation the sacred obligation to engage in prayer. In his elucidation of Jesus' words, "Truly,

truly, I say to you, if you ask anything of the Father, He will give it to you in My name" (John 16:23), he interprets them to mean that "Christ commands the disciples to pray." More than that, the Lord takes them to task for their neglect of prayer, pointing up the seriousness of his demand for "prayer as the true worship and work proper to Christians."

"Consider this command well," he continues solemnly, "and impress it on your consciousness, so that you will not think that you may pray or not pray at your discretion, as though it were not a sin if you did not pray but were sufficient to let others pray. No, you must know that God has earnestly enjoined prayer under pain of incurring His greatest disfavor and punishment, just as He commanded you not to have any other gods, not to blaspheme or misuse the name of God but to confess and proclaim, to praise and to extol it. And he who transgresses this command must know that he is no Christian and no member of God's kingdom."[50] God has every right to be angry with idolaters, blasphemers and those who scorn his Word. Indeed he inflicts punishment upon those who ignore his commandments and transgress them. Surely no one who claims to believe in God should therefore assume that he can disregard the commandment to pray with impunity.

Similarly the words of Christ, "Ask, and you will receive, that your joy may be full" (John 16:24), are both command and promise. Christ demands that we pray, that we obey his call to prayer. "And just as it is the purpose of Christ's promise and assurance to make us eager and willing, so this command should constrain and compel us. If I want to show my love for Christ and be obedient to Him, I have an obligation to pray, no matter how unworthy I may be...."[51] The mandate to pray cannot be circumvented. It is clearly set before the followers of Jesus Christ as both a privilege and a responsibility. That is why Luther also pleads for regular devotions such as praying at stated times in the morning and in the evening and not only when we are in dire need.[52]

Combined with the command to pray is the necessity of prayer. Since God knows what we need and what will be of benefit to us we might be tempted to conclude that even without our praying God will look after our needs. The assumption of such an attitude is wrong. Quoting the words of Augustine, "He who made you without you does not want to save you without you," Luther calls attention to God's *modus operandi*. We have a formidable variety of duties to perform so that we are in fact to apply the Apostle Paul's expression, "workers together with God" (2 Corinthians 6:1) to ourselves. While God has made us human beings out of clay without our assistance, it has been his good pleasure to propagate the human race through us as husbands and wives. We thus cooperate with him in the creative process. In a similar way he employs the ministry of the Word to teach and enlighten human hearts and to establish his kingdom on earth. God did not have to employ these means, but he freely chose to do so.

> For this reason He has established the external ministry and has instituted the sacraments. He is able to forgive sins without Baptism, but He does not do so; for He wants

us human beings to have a share in His workings. Therefore it would be the height of ingratitude to despise these. You must have the same convictions about prayer. For this is God's ordered will: He wants to be entreated, and to those who entreat Him he wants to give the Holy Spirit and everything they need.[53]

It is incumbent upon us to obey God's will. It is his will that we pray and any hesitation on our part to do this constitutes doubting him. Doubt vitiates prayer. We then become fainthearted in our praying. As a consequence, perceiving ourselves to be less gifted than Paul, Peter and others, we also become terrified with our unworthiness. So we draw the conclusion that we are undeserving and cannot obtain anything from God. Our faith and fervor diminish and become lukewarm, causing us to hesitate in keeping up our habit of praying and even expressing murmuring and discontent. "For who is worthy to speak with the Lord?" asks Luther in order to reply persuasively, "Therefore let it be enough for us that we have been called to faith through the Word, have been taught by the Word of God, and for this reason are part of the church, which has the definite command to pray."[54] Our unworthiness dare never become a decisive hindrance to praying in the face of God's command to do so. Rather we should hold fast to the promise that God desires to do for us what we are asking of him in prayer with reverent hearts.

Neglect of prayer incurs God's displeasure and wrath for the simple reason that his command to pray is disregarded. Trusting in him, we should arouse our sluggish hearts and pray boldly and confidently, assured that God will give us what we are asking for. If he should not give us what we are praying for, he will give us something better because the earnest and ardent prayer of his believing people is never in vain. Lot prayed for his deliverance when God was about to destroy Sodom and Gomorrah, and God heard his prayer. The answer he received to his prayer has consequently become a source of comfort to the godly. They, too, should pray when they are in danger and hope for the divine deliverance.[55]

CHAPTER TWO

THE INVITATION TO PRAYER

"Every word of God terrifies and comforts, hurts and heals; it breaks down and builds up; it plucks up and plants again; it humbles and exalts (Jeremiah 1:10)."[1] The truth of this assertion about God's Word, says Luther, is grasped only by faith. On the one hand, when we utter the petition in the Lord's Prayer, "Thy kingdom come," we recognize in our situation here on earth that God's kingdom has not yet come. Seriously pondering this reality, believing and pious hearts are appalled and grieved. God is robbed of his kingdom in us and we are the ones "who impair and obstruct" it. In his justice God would have every right to condemn us as his enemies and despoilers of his kingdom. Besides, we ourselves are held captive to sin and eternal death by powerful foes. On the other hand, the petition also contains a promise because Jesus as Lord instructs us to pray this petition for our salvation. "Those who confess that they impede God's kingdom and pray sorrowfully that this kingdom might still come to them, will, because of their penitence and prayer, be pardoned by God, when he would otherwise rightly punish them."[2] So in the dramatic contest between God's kingdom of light, righteousness, love and power and the kingdom of darkness and ultimate ruin the petition, "Thy kingdom come," is a promise of freedom from sin "when all our members, talents and powers are subject to God and are employed in his service, enabling us to say with Paul, 'I live, but it is no longer I but Christ who lives in me' [Galatians 2:20]. . . . That comes to pass when we are ruled not by sin, but only by Christ and his grace."[3] We cannot initate or come into this kingdom. It must come to us, even as "Christ came to us from heaven to earth; we did not ascend from earth into heaven to him."[4]

GOD'S PROMISES CONNECTED WITH PRAYER

Everything depends upon the promise of God or of Christ when we bring our prayers and petitions to him. "First, we must have a promise or a pledge from God. We must reflect on this promise and remind God of it, and in that way be emboldened to pray with confidence. If God had not enjoined us to pray and had not promised fulfillment, no creature would be able to obtain so much as a kernel of grain despite all his petitions."[5] The promise of God makes prayer efficacious and meaningful. Never dare we base any of our prayers on our own worthiness or virtue. Rather it is "solely by reason of the boundless mercy of God, who, by anticipating all our prayers and desires, induces us through his gracious promise and assurance to petition and to ask so that we might learn how much more he provides for us and how he is more willing to give than we to take or to seek [Ephesians 3:20]."[6] At the same time we dare not

25

doubt the validity of the promise. Our faith must be firm in order that the promise might find fulfillment in our lives. A cheerful reliance on the divine promise and a ready obedience to God's command to pray must characterize the petitions we bring to him. Doubting the fulfillment of what God has promised when one prays or even praying without passionate concern makes the prayer ineffectual. Such a person "destroys his own prayer and labors in vain."[7]

While prayer is recognized by Luther as an arduous labor in which we should engage with energetic concern, he also alleges that "the Christian's prayer is easy, and it does not cause hard work. For it proceeds in faith on the basis of the promise, and it presents its need from the heart."[8] The attitude in which one prays, namely, in the spirit of faith makes prayer a joyous undertaking, since such praying is prompted by faith in the promise of God. Or as Luther expressed it in another context, "Thus our prayer must, in real and sincere humility, take no account of ourselves; it must rely solely and confidently on the promise of grace, in the firm trust that God will hear us, as he has commanded us to pray and has promised to hear us."[9] The divine promise is noted as a fundamental component in our praying. We should concentrate on what God has promised, not looking at what we are before God but rather fixing our attention on the divine mercy and its manifestation in creation and redemption.

In Christ God's promise of grace has found its most consummate expression. That is why Luther urges that "you must also consider the promise contained in Christ's words: 'Truly, truly, I say to you, if you ask anything of the Father, He will give it to you in My name.' Lay hold of these words, and impress them on your heart." Jesus not only makes the promise that he will hear our prayers but also confirms his promise with an oath. He does this to confront us with our sluggishness and apathy in bringing our prayers to him and to impel us to begin to pray from the heart. "I say that in all fairness we should blush with shame before ourselves and really fear God's terrible judgment if we attach so little importance both to His command and to His solemn promise and allow them to fall on deaf ears. It will do no good to excuse yourself and say: 'I really did not know whether I was worthy' or 'I lacked the desire, and it was inconvenient for me' or 'I had to attend to other business.' "[10] The promise of the Word makes the practice of prayer an inescapably important privilege and responsibility in the lives of Christians. Failure to pray can therefore be blamed only on us and our unwillingness to be rightly motivated and empowered by Christ's promise of grace.

In his exposition of Psalm 51, referred to earlier, Luther made it clear that David's prayer was not directed to the absolute God, who is unknown and unknowable in his power and purpose. "He is speaking," explains Luther, "with the God of his fathers, with the God whose promises he knows and whose mercy he has felt." David was praying to God as he had veiled himself in the kind of mask, or face, that revealed his promise of mercy, forgiveness, and help to his people Israel. "This is the reason why the Prophets depended so upon God's promises in their prayers, because the promises include Christ and make God not our judge or enemy, but a God who is kind and well disposed to us, who wants to restore to life and save the condemned."[11] As a result of God's self-revelation through Moses and the prophets and finally fully through Jesus Christ his redeeming purpose of forgiveness and love became fully known. His promises in Christ reveal his heart and will and mind to us as human beings. That is why, clothed in the person of Jesus, God draws near to us with his promises of help and mercy so that we can come to him in prayer and count on receiving what we need both for body and spirit. As David had "taken hold of God the Promiser with the help of the Spirit and known that in God there remained a hope of forgiveness for sinners," so the conscience troubled by sin must take refuge in the promises of God which are "broadcast everywhere, even in the Law and the Decalog."[12] This fact causes Luther to make the comforting assertion, "Whenever we are stung and vexed in our conscience because of sins, let us simply turn our attention from sin and wrap ourselves in the bosom of God who is called Grace and Mercy, not doubting at all that He wants to show grace and mercy to miserable and afflicted sinners, just as He wants to show wrath and judgment to hardened sinners. This is true theology, which this verse of the psalm also manifests when it says, 'According to Thy abundant mercy blot out my transgressions.' "[13]

In a real sense God's promises, made known throughout the Scriptures and supremely and fully in Jesus Christ, are the true foundation for faith and prayer. Without the promises of God all certainty and hope would vanish, making prayer for forgiveness, new life, and help a futile cry of anguish lacking assurance and genuine comfort. Furthermore, the promises of God come to us under the mask of his Word, through which he has freely elected to reveal the liberating power and renewing purpose of his saving love to humankind.

PRAYER AND VOCATION

In order to be able to pray in a spirit of trust and obedience we have to rely on God's promise and disregard our own unworthiness. Then, as Luther puts it, you can put your petitions "in His lap joyfully and confidently. But above all, be sure that you really believe in Christ and that you have a proper occupation, one that pleases God, so that you are not like the world, which does not care about its occupation but only about the vices and villainy that it goes right on planning day and night."[14] Genuine prayer is here linked by Luther to a vocation in life in which one can serve God with a clear conscience. If one engages in some pursuit that is morally questionable and not defensible in the light of God's will made known in his Word, one has no right to seek God's help in prayer "vigorously and trustfully." Therefore, serving God in a vocation of which he approves gives us the necessary courage and confidence with which to approach God in prayer. "If we know God has obligated us to serve in our vocation we also know that he is our ultimate security. This feeling of being in his care is not the motive for the fulfillent of our vocational duty but is granted to us because, together with the demand God makes, we also experience his gracious providence."[15]

29

Because we believe in God's merciful care in accordance with Christ's teaching, we also pray for help and guidance in our vocation and count on God's help. It was for this reason that Luther faulted the peasants. They were not willing to desist from using force in their demands which they made of their lords and princes instead of trusting in God in their particular vocation. He told them in his *Admonition to Peace*,

> If you were Christians you would stop threatening and resisting with fist and sword. Instead, you would continually abide by the Lord's Prayer and say, "Thy will be done," and "Deliver us from evil, Amen" [Matthew 6:10,13]. The psalms show many examples of genuine saints taking their needs to God and complaining to him about them. They seek help from God; they do not try to defend themselves or to resist evil. That kind of prayer would have been more help to you, in all your needs, than if the world were full of people on your side. This would be especially true if, besides that, you had a good conscience and the comforting assurance that your prayers were heard....
>
> You have heard above that the gospel teaches Christians to endure and suffer wrong and pray to God in every need. You, however, are not willing to suffer, but like heathen, you want to force the rulers to conform to your impatient will. You cite the children of Israel as an example, saying that God heard their crying and delivered

them [Exodus 6:5-7]. Why then do you not follow the example that you cite? Call upon God and wait until he sends you a Moses, who will prove by signs and wonder that he was sent from God.[16]

Luther believed that the peasants had not sufficiently demonstrated their trust in God by means of prayer and patient negotiation with the princes. "Prayer is a positive action through which new and revolutionary ways are opened, for it brings into the earthly situation the God who is free from all external orders. The end of persevering prayer is to call in God, who turns the world upside down."[17] It was in this sense that Luther called upon the peasants to resort to prayer in their specific calling in life, even while he showed real empathy with their economic and social plight. The path of violence was not the one to be trodden by them because such a course of action could not be justified in the light of the call of God's word to be subject to the existing authorities (Romans 13:1ff.).

Whatever our vocation in life, suffering, difficulties and misunderstandings that are apt to occur in the pursuit of our responsibilities should drive us to prayer. The joy and assurance with which we can engage in prayer at such times are based on our faith in God's forgiveness and love by which we are justified in his sight. We therefore have the privilege to invoke God's support and blessing upon our various callings in life.

Luther rejected the false fatalism which was upheld and practiced by the Turks and which led them to say, "What can I do? What is the use of praying?

What does it help to worry? If it is predestined, it will happen."[18] We do not know what has been predestined, but are commanded to act on the basis of what we know.

> For that reason God has given us his word
> so that we should know what we are to do
> and not act on the basis of ignorance. The
> rest we have to leave to God and hold to our
> duty, vocation, and office. God, and he
> alone, knows what is to be. You are not sup-
> posed to know. . . .
> We must be guided according to our calling,
> not according to that which we may think is
> predestined and about which we are in the
> dark and know nothing for certain.[19]

We must arm ourselves "with the weapons of prayer," seeking God's help and strength in order to be able to endure suffering and to perform our duties. Specifically, a preacher in his calling has a two-fold task. He has the responsibility of teaching his people what is right and good; and before God he has the duty of praying that he may do what is right and win a victory over temptation and all wrong. The Word of God becomes the basis for this dual task of his.[20] A prince or ruler, too, is charged in his vocation with the arduous task of governing his subjects. Since he needs much insight and wisdom in doing this, he must learn to depend on God and pray for skill and a right judgment in order that he may rule his subjects wisely. He has to put his trust in God at all times, praying earnestly for the needed ability to govern his people in the spirit of Christian service.[21]

Prayer, according to Luther, is a revolutionary power in our various callings. At the same time, however, it is never to be substituted for the work which our diverse vocations demand. "He who turns to God in prayer for help from above, without doing all he can with the help of the outward gifts God has given us, is putting God to the test and cannot expect his prayers to be heard."[22] Prayer is not meant to become a substitute for action, even though it is an indispensable part of the Christian life. Prayer is designed to empower a person to do what is pleasing to God, namely, to help others in their need and to serve them in one's vocation. "For Christ at the last day will not ask how much you have prayed, fasted, pilgrimaged, done this or that for yourself, but how much good you have done to others, even to the very least [Matthew 25:40,45]."[23]

Guided by God's Word, we are to come together and bend our knees in prayer before him. We have been instructed not only by his promises but also by examples from the Scriptures that God wants to do for us what we earnestly desire of him in prayer. We should therefore never let our disposition to pray flag. "To be sure, God does everything; but we, too, must do what belongs to our calling. He gives bread to nourish and preserve the body; but He gives it to him who labors, sows, reaps, etc."[24] So we must faithfully do our part in our vocation, praying for his blessing and help and performing the required labor.

For Luther the three foundational orders or "truly religious institutions" in the world were the home, the church, and the civil government or state.[25] Parents have the responsibility of caring for their children and the household in their calling; bishops and pastors are called upon to administer the affairs of the church; and princes, judges, magistrates, and councilors are persons placed in positions of rule and authority in the state. How can these individuals carry out their several responsiblities best?

> Should nothing at all be done, and should all managing be shunned entirely? Not at all. Rather let everyone diligently and faithfully do his duty which has been committed to him by God. But let him beware of relying on his own strength or his own wisdom and of considering himself such a great man that everything should be directed in accordance with what he counsels. For it is incurable and damnable rashness and arrogance on my part when I claim to be such a person and such an extraordinary man that I can manage the state, the home, and the church wisely and properly. But if you are a judge, a bishop, or a prince, you should not feel ashamed to fall on your knees and say: "Lord God, Thou hast appointed me as prince, judge, head of the household, and pastor of the church. Therefore guide and teach me, give me counsel, wisdom, strength to attend successfully to the office committed to me."[26]

Indeed, a person should humbly learn to acknowledge his weakness before God and ask him for enlightenment and guidance. Persons summoned to govern should not presume to possess perfect knowledge in everything. Rather, they should learn to acknowledge that they are instruments through which God himself rules the people. Only in that way can they govern well and wisely. "But if they follow their own counsels and their own thoughts, they do nothing properly. No, then they disturb and confuse everything. Therefore one must take refuge in prayer, set forth the difficulty of the office to God, and say: 'Our Father who art in heaven, etc., give me wisdom that sits by Thy throne' (Wisdom of Solomon 9:4)."[27]

Above all, a person who has been called to rule or administer the affairs in the church should pray in this manner:

> Lord God, Thou hast appointed me as bishop and pastor in the church. Thou seest how unfit I am to administer such a great and difficult office, and if it had not been for Thy help, I would long since have ruined everything. Therefore I call upon Thee. Indeed, I desire to consecrate my mouth and heart to this ministry. I shall teach the people, and I myself shall learn and shall meditate diligently on Thy Word. Use me as Thy instrument. Only do not forsake me; for if I am left alone, I will certainly bring it all to destruction.[28]

Luther points to Moses as a magnificent example of a leader who depended wholly on God's mercy and help. Turning the reins of leadership back to God, he even declines to do what the Lord has commanded unless God himself goes before him and his people.

Therefore he says trustingly in prayer to God: "If Thy presence will not go with me, do not carry us up from here" (Exodus 33:15).

"Thus I, too," confesses Luther, "often cast the keys at the feet of the Lord, as the German proverb puts it; that is, I turned back to Him the administrative office that had been committed to me. For this reason the matter had an outcome far different from what I had foreseen or thought. And if I had made some mistake, He Himself corrected it in accordance with His goodness and wisdom."[29]

In the matter of discharging the responsibility in one's vocation one should readily acknowledge one's dependence on God. Many of those who are entrusted with a particular calling in life fail to do so. It is evident, however, that they

> will never achieve anything without prayer. For governing is a divine power, and for this reason God calls all magistrates gods (cf. Psalm 82:6), not because of the creation but because of the administration which belongs to God alone. Consequently, he who is in authority is an incarnate god, so to speak. But if they force their way into the government of the church, the state, or the household rashly and without due preparation, exclude God, do not pray, and do not seek advice from God, but want to rule everything with their own counsels and strength, then it will eventually happen in the management of household affairs that an honorable and chaste wife will become a harlot of the worst kind and that the children will

degenerate and come into the power of the executioner. In the civil government that state will be thrown into confusion by insurrections, wars, robberies, and countless other perils. In the church, heresies, Epicurean contempt for the Word, desecration of the sacraments, etc., will arise. Why? Because such a head of a household, prince, or pastor does not recognize God as the Author of all counsel and government but by his presumption and arrogance destroys himself and others over whom he rules.[30]

Whatever our vocation in life, we must remember that as persons who work with God, or rather who let God work through us, we are God's instruments by means of which he desires to effect his good and gracious purpose in his created world. Prayer is such an integral part of letting God do his work through us that neglecting or overlooking its importance means inviting ultimate ruin and disaster in the vocation we have.

GIVING GOD THE GLORY

In 1519 Luther wrote *An Exposition of the Lord's Prayer for Simple Laymen.* In treating the first petition, "Hallowed be thy name," he notes first of all that it is "an infinitely profound petition" if it is prayed from the heart. Indeed, when this is done "God becomes everything and man becomes nothing."[31] In fact every subsequent petition in the Lord's Prayer according to Luther's observation serves the same purpose of hallowing God's name. If God's name is hallowed by us, everything else that we do is done well.

Prayer is in itself the acknowledgement of God as the Giver of everything, and we glorify him by praying that his name might be honored by us. "For by honoring God we bring him the first and the last and the highest offering within our power; nor does he seek and ask for more. Moreover, we cannot give God anything else, for it is he who gives us everything else. But he does claim for himself this honor, namely, that we acknowledge and witness in our words and songs, our lives and deeds, in all that we do and suffer, that everything is of God. . . . "[32]

The deeds of his people, in whom God lives and works, bring honor and glory to him because they ascribe everything to him. Thus they put the petition of hallowing God's name into practice, giving honor to God and suffering dishonor themselves if need be. But human arrogance is responsible for refusing to hallow God's name. It is the fountainhead of all sin. So when arrogance is destroyed sin cannot live and do its harm. However, since none of us as human beings are without pride and we without exception covet honor for ourselves, it is highly necessary and salutary that we pray "Hallowed be thy name" and so learn to give God the honor due his name.

In all troubles and infirmities of life we should invoke God's holy name, not forgetting it when our consciences trouble us and when we face death. Rather we should use all our powers and possessions to glorify and honor God. In our prayers we ought not to ask for anything either temporal or eternal that does not serve God's glory and bring honor to his name. Our conduct should prove that we are true children of God who rightly call him our Father and who bring him "all psalms and prayers of praise, honor, and thanksgiving."[33]

The word "to hallow" has the meaning "to praise, extol, and honor" the name of God in our words and deeds. Luther sees a great need for this kind of praying because it implies that, having the Word of God, we should live in accordance with its directives. So whenever this petition is prayed with a believing heart we can "be sure that God is pleased. For there is nothing he would rather hear than to have his glory and praise exalted above everything else and his Word taught in its purity and cherished and treasured."[34]

It is when we fail to put our trust in God, when we doubt his promises and do not pray believingly that we rob him of his honor and of his reputation as one who is faithful and true.[35] Persons who lack faith fail disastrously in prayer. Their petitions are futile. But those who trustingly bring their prayers to God in the sincere desire to honor his name also give him all glory and praise. That is why Luther uttered this prayer: "Confirm in us, Lord God, what you are doing, and complete your work, which you have begun in us, to your glory. Amen."[36] Thus God's glory was both the point of departure and the ultimate goal of prayer for Luther.

PART TWO

PRAYER AS COMMUNICATION WITH GOD THROUGH CHRIST

CHAPTER THREE

THE BASIS OF PRAYER

In and through the person of Jesus Christ we are assured of God's gracious regard for us. God's grace in Christ is the source and center of our trust in him and the basis for our prayers to him. Because God is gracious and we know that we would perish without his good gifts and favor we come to him with our needs and desires in prayer. Without his sustaining and renewing presence and power in our lives and in the world about us, we acknowledge by faith that we would eventually experience utter extinction. We therefore exult in his grace, in his unmerited favor and great compassion. Luther enlarges on the meaning of God's grace in his exposition of the Magnificat in this way: "In giving us the gifts He gives only what is His, but in His grace and His regard of us He gives His very self. In the gifts we touch His hand; but in His gracious regard we receive His heart, spirit, mind, and will." Luther then proceeds to clarify the distinction he has made. "Where God's gracious will is, there are also His gifts; but on the other hand, where His gifts are, there is not also His gracious will." He therefore concludes: "Thus God would not have His true children put their trust in His goods and gifts, spiritual or temporal, however great they be, but in His grace and in Himself, yet without despising the gifts."[1]

GOD'S GRACE IN CHRIST

In his grace God is completely and unreservedly available to us, bestowing upon us his forgiveness and love and opening the way for unhindered communication with him in our prayer life. In Christ God has come to us in the fullness of his love and gives himself to us as our God, our Father, our Savior and our Lord. This self-giving of God in the birth, life, death and resurrection of his Son takes on reality and meaning in the life of humanity and in our individual and corporate lives by virtue of the Holy Spirit's work through the witness of the Word of God. The divine largess in creation and redemption becomes known, haveable and graspable when with the open hand of faith one receives God's grace offered in Jesus Christ through Word and Spirit. Christ's work of redemption is complete; the divine grace has been fully revealed in him; and the good news of this saving event has to be made known. "In order that this treasure might not be buried but put to use and enjoyed, God has caused the Word to be published and proclaimed, in which he has given the Holy Spirit to offer and apply to us this treasure of salvation."[2]

In the three articles of the Apostles' Creed Luther sees an apt summation of what the grace of God means for human lives. "In these three articles God himself has revealed and opened to us the most profound depths of his fatherly heart, his sheer, unutterable love," comments Luther. "He created us for this very purpose, to redeem and sanctify us. Moreover, having bestowed upon us everything in heaven and on earth, he has given us his Son and his Holy Spirit, through whom he brings us to himself."[3] The way to such faith and confidence in God's gracious will and purpose is the person of Jesus Christ. God's grace would remain unknown to us if it were not for Christ's earthly life, his death and resurrection. He mirrors his heavenly Father's heart. He discloses God's mercy and forgiving love. Apart from him God's true nature and purpose remain obscure and threatening. Moreover, without the Holy Spirit's witness in and through the Word we would not be able to trust in God revealed in Christ.

The trinitarian focus for our faith forms the solid basis for the divine grace which enables us to address our prayers to God. When we pray that God's kingdom might come to us, we therefore realize that it comes to us by God's grace alone. "We will never be able to come into this kingdom. Similarly, Christ came to us from heaven to earth; we did not ascend from earth into heaven to him."[4] Thus Luther acknowledges the indispensable necessity and priority of God's grace in all that pertains to being God's people and being privileged to pray to him as our Father. It is God's grace when the Word of God is communicated to us, simultaneously humbling us as sinners and exalting us as forgiven and justified people; "for the Word of God always works both judgment and righteousness."[5]

Interpreting the petition of the Lord's Prayer, "Give us this day our daily bread," spiritually during his early career in harmony with Augustine's exposition of it, Luther equates the grace of God with the bread of life. "The bread, the Word, and the food are none other than Jesus Christ our Lord himself. Thus he declares in John 6[:51], 'I am the living bread which came down from heaven to give life to the world.' So then, let no one be deceived by words or false appearances. Sermons and doctrines which do not bring and show Jesus Christ to us are not the daily bread and nourishment of our souls, nor will they help us in any need or trial."[6] As in the sermon, so in the sacrament of the Lord's Supper, Christ is received. "However," explains Luther, "this would not happen if Christ were not, at the same time, prepared and distributed through the Word."[7] Jesus Christ as true man and at the same time as the eternal Son, "begotten of the Father from eternity," is the personification of the divine grace in the Word and in the sacraments. Luther was completely Christocentric in his concept of grace and its indispensable necessity for faith and prayer.

"I believe that no one can believe in the Father and that no one can come to him by any ability, deeds, understanding, or anything that may be named in heaven or on earth [Ephesians 3:15]. Rather, this faith is possible only in and through Jesus Christ, his only Son, that is, through faith in his name and lordship."[8] For this reason Luther can ask God in prayer for help and grace and above all "a true and constant faith in Christ." Jesus Christ is the epitome of God's grace and therefore the one who enables us to pray with certainty and joy.

Although this grace is revealed by Jesus Christ, Luther also speaks of God the Father's grace and of the grace of the Holy Spirit. After stating that in a Christian's life there is a spirit of restlessness amid the greatest calm, namely, in God's grace and peace, he points out that the believer is never still or idle. "He constantly strives and struggles with all his might, as one who has no other object in life than to disseminate God's honor and glory among the people, that others may also receive such a Spirit of grace and through this Spirit also help him to pray. For wherever the Spirit of grace resides, there we can and dare, yes, must begin to pray."[9] The Holy Spirit as the Spirit of grace moves a person mightily to come before God in prayer. Possessed by the Spirit of grace, one relies altogether upon the totally unmerited love of God in Christ, our Lord, when one prays. Thus the divine grace must ever remain the true source and basis of the believer's cheerful confidence in his prayer life.

PRAYER AND CONFESSION

According to Luther there are three kinds of confession. First, there is the voluntary confession of our sins in the presence of a pastor or a fellow-believer in order that we might be assured of forgiveness for the sake of Jesus Christ. This is called private confession. The two other kinds of confession have to do with confessing our sins to God alone in prayer and to our neighbor alone and asking for forgiveness. These last two types of confession are articulated in the fifth petition of the Lord's Prayer, "Forgive us our sins, as we forgive those who sin against us." "Indeed," explains Luther, "the whole Lord's Prayer is nothing else than such a confession. For what is

47

our prayer but a confession that we neither have nor do what we ought and a plea for grace and a happy conscience? This kind of confession should and must take place incessantly as long as we live. For this is the essence of a genuinely Christian life, to acknowledge that we are sinners and to pray for grace."[10]

The confession of sin in prayer before God is the lifelong obligation of his people. Such a practice is in harmony with the spirit and meaning of the first of Luther's *Ninety-five Theses*, "When our Lord and Master Jesus Christ said, 'Repent' [Matthew 4:7], he willed the entire life of believers to be one of repentance."[11] There is thus never a time in our lives when repentance and the confession of sin are out of place. "God looks with favor only on those who sincerely confess that they dishonor his name and ever desire that it may be hallowed."[12] It is as wayfaring pilgrims in this world that we acknowledge constantly in prayer that we are plagued by weaknesses and sins and so ask for forgiveness. By God's grace we begin to live a godly life. However, as soon as we start doing God's will, we encounter the resistance of our old nature. "One's own will, inborn from Adam, contends with all our members against the good impulses. Then the grace in our hearts cries to God for help against this Adam and says, 'Thy will be done.' "[13] Confessing our sins to God in prayer becomes the means of securing strength to resist wrong and to follow the good. God wants to help us in the fight against all sin and evil as often as we pray, "Thy will be done."

"The righteous are wise and well aware of the purpose of the divine will, even though it involves all kinds of adversity. They also know what their proper attitude over against this must be. They know that no enemy has ever been put to flight by a fleeing person."[14] Honestly confessing one's sins in prayer to God arms a person for the conflict because one acknowledges sin and failure and learns to depend more and more on the grace and power of God in facing the enemies of Christian living.

Luther sees two elements in true repentance. First, there is the knowledge of sin which causes a person to fear God. Second, repentance implies the recognition of grace which prompts us to trust in the divine mercy. Because of our sinful condition we are tempted to put off praying. On the one hand, we may become confused, believing that we should delay praying until we can find something worthy in us that will give us confidence to do so. On the other hand, we may look around for human counsel in our predicament, hoping that our own efforts at making satisfaction for our sins will provide a satisfactory basis for bringing our prayers to God. "This is the constant belief of our nature," warns Luther, "but it is highly dangerous. It encourages our minds to trust in our own righteousness and to think that we can please God with our own works. This is a blasphemous presumption of our own merits against the merits of Christ. Since we are born in sins, it follows that we shall never pray unless we pray before we feel that we are pure of all sins."[15]

We have to dispel these false notions about ourselves. Though we are in the midst of sins, we should not put off praying. The prayer for mercy is never spoken by those who are pure, but by those who feel their sin and need. Luther himself confesses that "this is a very bitter battle, that in the very feeling of sin a mind can be aroused to cry to God, 'Have mercy on me.' From my own example I have sometimes learned that prayer is the most difficult of all works, I who teach and command others! Therefore I do not profess to be a master of this work, but rather confess that in great danger I have often repeated the words very coldly, 'Have mercy on me, O God,' because I was offended by my unworthiness."[16]

Precisely when we feel our sins and lack of goodness we should pray for God's mercy. "God does not want the prayers of a sinner who does not feel his sins, because he neither understands nor wants what he is praying for."[17] In fact his prayer is an empty recital of words since he does not really mean what he says. He is like a beggar who is constantly crying out for alms. Then when the alms are offered to him be begins to brag about his supposed riches, namely, his poverty, clearly showing that he does not want the alms in the first place. It is only after the heart has been crushed by the hammer of the law and the judgment of God that a person prays with an upright spirit for the divine mercy. The Lord takes pleasure in those who are of a humble and contrite heart, fear him and plead for grace. "The whole of theological knowledge" is "that God gives grace to the humble (1 Peter 5:5)."[18] While it is not so difficult to call upon God to have mercy in general, it is the hardest of all prayers to add the particle "on me." Yet this is what the gospel would have us do. "This 'on me' hinders almost all our prayers, when it ought to be the only reason and highest occasion for praying."[19]

In Psalm 51 David asked the Lord to have mercy on him, and God showed him his mercy. He was praying to God who not only had mercy on him but who was also ready to grant the same mercy to all others who confessed their sins and sought forgiveness. He is the same God to all without distinction. He forgives sins and has mercy on all those who, like David, acknowledge their sin and pray to him for mercy.

On the basis of his ardent search for a gracious God Luther, in the course of his exposition of various books of Scripture, had recovered the biblical picture of the human being. When it emerged in its distinct outlines this picture was at variance with the scholastic theology of Ockham which Luther had embraced as a monk. Ockham called upon the individual believer to do what lay in him (*facere quod in se est*) so that he might thus dispose himself favorably for God's grace. But the scriptural witness and Luther's own experience did not square with this anthropological teaching. Nor was it in accord with the optimistic assessment of the human condition by the humanism of his day which held that a person had residual spiritual strength in coming to faith in the salvation offered by God in Jesus Christ.

While scholasticism attributed to the human being certain superior faculties controlled by reason, like the will and the intellect, it designated other faculties of his being as inferior which were ruled by sensuality with its passions and desires. Accordingly, sin appeared to stem almost exclusively from the sensual drives which subjected to temptation the superior intellectual faculties of a person. If in the inner core of one's being one gave assent to these sensual desires on the basis of one's own moral and reason-controlled will and carried them out, one fell into sin. If, however, one resisted these same desires successfully, one retained one's moral rectitude.

In teaching this kind of anthropology the philosophy of the ancient Greeks had been uncritically given a place in medieval scholastic theology, creating the impression as if the spiritual center of the human being was uncorrupted and as if a person could carry out satisfactory acts of love toward God and other humans on his own. It also appeared as if Christ had given his life on the cross solely for the sensual nature which had fallen prey to the sinful desires of the flesh rather than for the nobler rational and spiritual core of one's being.[20]

Luther rejected these doctrinal assertions of scholasticism about human nature, replacing them with the biblical teaching of the fall, according to which the human being in all of his faculties and powers is controlled by sin. There is no part of a person that can in any way prepare the way for God's coming to him. A fallen person is "as nothing" before God because he opposes the divine will and seeks to assert his own will in life. He is a rebel against God, loving himself and seeking himself in everything.[21]

The fall actualizes itself continually in the life of humanity. So we turn away from God, the Giver of all, in our unbelief and pride, seeking to live independently of him. We are indeed captive to the law of sin and death and our wills err unfailingly because the Spirit of God does not control them.

Consequently our natural knowledge of God is

never true knowledge, but always a distorted and false knowledge, causing us to construct a false picture of who we are before God. "Therefore the root and source of sin is unbelief and turning away from God," observes Luther, "just as, on the other hand, the source and root of righteousness is faith."[22]

Unbelief in its proud and rebellious spirit of independence from God controls us as fallen persons. As such we try to make ourselves lords and masters of God's creation, believing that we are accountable to no one but ourselves. This bleak picture of our sinfulness, of our revolt against God, of unbelief and total lostness was again clearly presented by Luther. On the basis of the biblical witness he depicted our actual situation before God. His persevering, arduous and prayerful study of God's Word had led him to the rediscovery of the truth about the human predicament. So he humbly and contritely confessed his own bondage to sin and death from which only Jesus Christ as Savior and Lord could free him.

The recognition and confession of sin before God are, however, not possible on the basis of our own insights and capabilities. The Word of God has to uncover our deep inner need, our innate sin. "With faith in this Word let us confess that this is the way things are, even though all nature should object, as object it must."[23] It is admittedly most difficult to accept something that we cannot analyze with our own intellects in all the dimensions of its depth and pervasiveness. Yet that is what we are called upon to do. Our proper understanding of Scripture depends on our believing the verdict of God's Word that we are sinners. "So we are not sinners because we commit this or that sin, but we commit them because we are sinners first. That is, a bad tree and a bad seed also bring forth bad fruit, and from a bad root only a bad tree can grow."[24] Our praying to God in spirit and in truth is predicated on the confession that in his Word the Lord has revealed to us who we are in his sight, namely, sinners, and that only by his mercy and forgiveness can we be made whole again. "Those who acknowledge their impurity in this way and cast themselves upon mercy will obtain mercy, because God is glorified by this confession and has promised forgiveness to those who trust in Him."[25]

Luther calls those counterfeit saints who claim that God loves them even while they are subject to his wrath. However, those who hear in the Word of God that they are sinners and that only God is righteous doubt God's love and are afraid of his wrath. This is a natural deduction on their part because when human nature recognizes its sin it naturally concludes that God hates sinners. Luther labels this "our wisdom." In Psalm 51 we are taught the heavenly wisdom "that God does not want to reject but to love true sinners, while those who attack this confession and do not want to be sinners are liars, and God hates them. Why should a sinner be timid and fear wrath, since God sent His Son to render satisfaction for sins?" Luther, having raised this question, answers it forthrightly by stating that since God has established his righteousness in Christ for us there is no need of arguing about it. Therefore God "requires us to acknowledge that we are sinners. This acknowledgement or confession is the truth, not a philosophical truth which reason hears and sees, but a theological and hidden truth which only the Spirit sees and hears."[26]

In the parable of the Pharisee and the tax collector, Luther reminds us that the Pharisee makes mention of his fasts and his virtues, believing that these outward acts of seeming goodness will please God. But he is mistaken because God loves the truth in secret. The possession of civic honesty and goodness on the part of a person is not at all the determining factor in the sight of God. What we are outwardly will not commend us to God. It is our inner attitude, which has to do with theological truth, that is, the truth before the Lord who searches the hearts, that is decisive. "That hidden truth and wisdom must be present, that we confess our sins and yet become bold when we feel death, conscience, and the arrows of the devil, and that we say: 'Thou dost love truth in secret. That is, Thou dost love those who confess their sins and believe the promise that Thou dost want to be merciful to them.' "[27]

In his comments on Psalm 51 Luther makes the daring claim that a godly person will feel sin more than grace, wrath more than divine favor, judgment more than redemption. An ungodly person by contrast feels almost nothing of the divine wrath. In his smugness he discounts the concept of wrath altogether as though the kind of God who vindicates his righteousness does not really exist. Only where religion is evaluated solely in terms of outward appearances does this false view of God obtain. "On the other hand, the more a godly man feels his weakness, the more earnest he is in prayer. With this wisdom there simultaneously begins continuous prayer. Because the feeling of sin does not cease, sighing and prayers do not cease, asking that this wisdom may be made perfect."[28] Only if there is an inwardly upright confession of sin before God, can we begin by faith to pray for forgiveness in an acceptable way and, being in the truth through the work of the Spirit, we learn to pray continuously because of the ongoing consciousness of being sinners and of the constant need of grace. Although we possess the forgiveness of sins, we continue to sigh and pray for that forgiveness throughout our lives. The reason for unceasing prayer in the lives of the godly is that their hearts are not satisfied with the first fruits of the Spirit (Romans 8:23). They want to have the Spirit in his fullness.

Luther rightly links with the confession of sin and of unworthiness before God in prayer the confession of faith in God before the world. "After justification, when you believe the promise of the forgiveness of sins and eternal life and possess it by faith, then the next and continuing work is to give thanks to God and preach these blessings of His. Because the world sets itself against this with all its force and Satan does not stop trying to take this proclamation away from us by throwing up various discomforts, therefore in the preceding verse David prayed for a brave spirit which despises dangers and courageously gives 'testimony of Christ,' as Luke says of the Apostles."[29] Prayer is called for if we want to confess our faith before others in the world.

It is a pious and precious work in the eyes of God when sinners are converted to him. This work of confessing Christ and bearing witness to his name is fraught with danger. First of all, it can be carried out only by those whom the Holy Spirit confirms in their faith and makes constant in their confession. Secondly, the work of making a good confession of faith before those who do not yet believe is a very significant undertaking because of the fruit which it bears. "Therefore, even though the dangers of this work could frighten us away, its usefulness should urge us on, because it is impossible for the Word of God to be preached without fruit. Although not all are converted, still there are some who are changed from sinners to believers and are saved."[30] In order that we might take part in this important work of planting the Word of God far and wide, we have to undergird such efforts with prayer and depend on the empowering presence of the Spirit. Thus others will be brought to faith in Christ. Such a confession of our faith before others follows a confession of our sins before God.

Finally, Luther joins the public confession of faith to the praise of God. When we read in Psalm 51:15, "O Lord, Thou wilt open my lips, and my mouth will announce thy praise," the prophetic writer "is not dealing with a private conversation between God and the sinner, but with the whole church, the ministry and the ministers and the whole people of God."[31] Those of us who have been justified by faith have no alternative other than confessing the mercy of God in public. "Therefore, those who want to give due praise to a work that is great and worthy of a Christian man, . . . let them praise this, the confession of the name of the Lord before the world. For this is the virtue of virtues and the highest and hardest work."[32] When the risk of publicly confessing Christ and making known his saving power is taken by believers, they need the gracious help of God's Spirit as they offer this prayer, "O Lord, open my lips." For Luther, Romans 10:10 states the conclusion of the whole matter. "Faith cannot be otherwise; it always confesses what it believes."[33]

PRAYER IN CHRIST'S NAME

What did Christ mean when he directed his followers to pray to the Father in his name? Luther interpreted this request as a way of making plain that we should in no way take account of ourselves. In fact we should look away from ourselves and rely solely on the promising God. Christ "wants to teach us that no real prayer is possible without faith and that without Christ no one is able to utter a single word of prayer that is valid before God and acceptable to Him."[34] Anyone who appears before God in prayer in the belief that God will take into account that person's merits or holiness is praying in vain. Instead of wanting to receive something from God, that individual wants to offer something to God and so oblige him to give him a reward. But God refuses to hear the prayer of anyone who does not come in the name of Christ and does not throw himself entirely on God's pure mercy. It is for Christ's sake that God looks favorably upon the petitions we bring to him in prayer.

God is gracious and hears our prayers only because we offer them in Jesus' name. In addition to making the request that prayers should be addressed to the Father in his name, Jesus utters the astounding words, "Whatever you ask of me, I will do." By saying this he is making known who he is and what he can do. "What a peculiar speech from this Man," comments Luther, "to clothe such arrogance in such simple words! For with these words He lets it be clearly understood that He is the true, almighty God, coequal with the Father." If this would not have been the case, Christ would not have made such a bold statement. His words, therefore, are tantamount to asserting that he himself is God and possesses the divine power to grant what his disciples have prayed for in his name. "But now Christ claims all this for Himself and says: 'I will order no one else to give you what you ask for. No, I Myself will do this.' Consequently, He must be the one who can supply all our wants. He must be mightier than the devil, sin, death, the world, and all creatures."[35]

Christ was not only the one who represented God on earth but who was in fact, in the words of the Nicene Creed, "God from God, Light from Light, true God from true God." For Luther the Scripture testified to the complete deity of Christ. For that reason Jesus possesses power and authority which are above any and every might and rule in the universe. To be sure, there were the apostles and the prophets, like Elijah and Elisha, who raised people from the dead by means of prayer.

> But the power to grant and to do such things, to save from any distress of sin and death, is not vested in them. Christ, however, takes to Himself all the power and might of the Divine Majesty and sums up in one sentence everything we should ask God for. He does not say: "If you pray for gold or silver or for anything that man, too, could

give you;" but He says: "Whatever you ask," barring nothing. We know, of course, what we must ask God for. We must ask not only for this beggarly earthly pittance, that is, for all the needs of this temporal life; but we should pray for deliverance from all present and future misery, from sin, death, and the grave, and that we may be made just, holy, free, alive, and glorious. And since Christ bids us pray for all this and promises to grant it, He must be true God.[36]

Our great distinction as Christians is that we have been called and chosen by Christ through his word. We are by reason of this call to discipleship victors over sin, death and the power of the devil. Connected with the bestowal of the privilege of being Jesus' friends and followers is the call to servanthood. "In the second place, we are also to be His servants and lend a hand in spreading His kingdom, to do much good." This responsibility involves the danger of defamation and persecution by and in the world. In the face of this fact a third item is added by Jesus who says: "So that whatever you ask the Father in My name, He may give it to you" (John 15:16). Luther explains that "through this grace in Christ we not only become God's friends through Him and acquire God as our Father; but our election also enables us to ask Him for whatever we need and to be assured that it will be given to us." With cheerful confidence we can now come to God in prayer, certain that he will hear us and will also give us what we may need because we make our requests in faith and in Christ's name. "We have been ordained to the priestly office.

Hence we can and must step before God joyfully, as we bring both our own need and that of others before Him, assured by His promise that our prayers will be heard and that He will say yea and amen to them."[37]

Since we have been chosen by Christ and have been directed to bear much fruit in his kingdom, we have been promised the resources we need through believing prayer in his name. The promise of Christ to answer prayers made "in my name" is of pivotal importance to the Reformer. It makes prayer a joyful undertaking. To ask for something in Jesus' name "is the foundation upon which prayer must rest. These words give to prayer the good quality and the dignity that make it acceptable to God. They also free us from severe trials and from useless worries regarding our worthiness, worries that hinder our praying and frighten us more than anything else." In fact Jesus' words should embolden us and we should not be "worried about our own worthiness but should forget about both worthiness and unworthiness and base our prayers on Christ and pray in His name."[38]

All our prayers must be centered in Christ alone. Christendom as a whole prays in this way, concluding and sealing all its prayers with the deeply meaningful words, "through Jesus Christ, our Lord." "In this way it brings its offerings to God in faith."[39] There is no Christian who should fail to do likewise. In fact we should be ready to fall upon our knees when we are seized with feelings of unworthiness and cling to Christ, making our prayer in dependence on him alone and asking God to hear it for Christ sake. There will then be no uncertainty or doubt but utter confidence that our prayer has come before God and has already been granted, for it was offered in the name of Christ, which is in complete conformity with Jesus' word and directive and therefore acceptable to God.

Prayer in Jesus' name is the distinctive mark of Christian worship, differentiating it from all other forms of worship in the world, even from the worship practiced in the Old Testament by the holy patriarchs. A newness inheres in the worship of God when prayers are offered in the name of Christ. For by reason of our faith in Jesus Scripture as a whole and the Psalms in particular are invested with a new meaning so that they ring new on our lips. As Savior and Lord, Jesus wants to remove all differences and disparity, unifying all believers and enabling them to join St. Paul in speaking of one God, one church, one faith, one prayer and worship, one Christ. "Anything that is to qualify as true prayer and worship must be stamped with the simple words, 'in My name.' . . . God will hear and acknowledge only what is presented in the name of Christ."[40]

CHAPTER FOUR

THE FOCUS FOR PRAYER

The sinner's justification by grace through faith in Christ is the centerpiece and heart of Luther's theology. This teaching epitomized for him the gospel of Jesus Christ. He spelled out the centrality of this teaching and its primary importance in the *Smalcald Articles* of 1537.

> The first and chief article is this, that Jesus Christ, our God and Lord, "was put to death for our trespasses and raised again for our justification" (Romans 4:25). He alone is "the Lamb of God, who takes away the sin of the world" (John 1:29). . . . Moreover, "all have sinned," and "they are justified by his grace as a gift, through the redemption which is in Christ Jesus, by his blood" (Romans 3:23-25).
>
> Inasmuch as this must be believed and cannot be obtained or apprehended by any work, law or merit, it is clear and certain that such faith alone justifies. . . . Nothing in this article can be given up or compromised, even if heaven and earth and things temporal should be destroyed. For as St. Peter says, "There is no other name under heaven

given among men by which we must be saved" (Acts 4:12). "And with his stripes we are healed" (Isaiah 53:5).[1]

PRAYER AND JUSTIFICATION

1. *Prayer and Forgiveness*

Luther's understanding of prayer is based on his concept of God, which in turn is derived from the central message of the gospel, our justification by grace through faith.[2] In its essence the doctrine on justification determines the nature and meaning of prayer because justification has to do with the establishment of a right relationship between God and ourselves. Therefore Luther considers the teaching on justification the genuine basis for prayer. Though one may have knowledge of all other doctrines of the Christian faith, real prayer becomes possible only by making this pivotal doctrine the core of one's faith and confession.[3]

It should be clearly understood that our justification before God for Christ's sake through faith is not a one-time event which automatically has its impact upon us for the rest of our lives; rather, it is a recurring phenomenon by which through faith in Jesus Christ we are forgiven and granted his righteousness ever anew in our particular situation in life in order that we might deepen and confirm this restored relationship with God through prayer, worship and service.[4]

Luther sees the act of justification as being twofold in its effect upon us as believers, namely, the bestowal of forgiveness by a gracious heavenly Father and the gift of renewal through the Holy Spirit.

There are the two parts of justification. The first is grace revealed through Christ, that through Christ we have a gracious God, so that sin can no longer accuse us, but our conscience has found peace through trust in the mercy of God. The second part is the conferring of the Holy Spirit with His gifts, who enlightens us against the defilements of spirit and flesh (2 Cor. 7:1). Thus we are defended against the opinions with which the devil seduces the whole world. Thus the true knowledge of God grows daily, together with other gifts, like chastity, obedience and patience. Thus our body and its lusts are broken so that we do not obey them.[5]

Luther calls the righteousness of Christ which is granted us by imputation an alien righteousness. It is a righteousness outside of ourselves (*extra nos*). "We should note diligently," states Luther, "that this purity is an alien purity, for Christ adorns and clothes us with His righteousness. So if you look at a Christian without the righteousness and purity of Christ, as he is in himself, even though he be most holy, you will find not only no cleanness, but what I might call diabolical blackness."[6] By faith we cling to Christ as our righteousness, a righteousness given us in baptism, through the hearing of the gospel and the believing of God's promises. Without baptism and the gospel and its promises we are bereft of all purity and are in bondage to sin. So if we are asked how we can be washed of the sin that clings to us and be made whiter than snow, the answer is this: "We should look at a man, not as he is in himself, but as he is in Christ. There you will find that believers are washed and cleansed by the blood of Christ. Who is so profane as to deny that the blood of Christ is most pure?" Can there still be uncertainty about a person's purity? "Because he still feels the remnants of sin in himself? But all purity must be this alien purity of Christ and His blood. It must not be our own, which we put on ourselves."[7] As believers we are children of God and heirs of the heavenly Father's kingdom because Christ alone is our righteousness and has granted all the privileges and rights to us as adopted sons and daughters of God.

Our justification before God requires nothing of us. God "simply wants the forgiveness of sins, which alone grants joy, to come only through the Word or only through hearing. For if you tortured yourself to death, if you shed your blood, if with ready heart you underwent and bore everything that is humanly possible — all this would not help you." Hearing the message of salvation alone brings joy. "This is the only way for the heart to find peace before God. Everything else leaves doubt in the mind."[8] "This whole procedure in justification is passive." We must do nothing and let God have his way with us. To consider ourselves righteous, or holy, we want to be justified actively by what we have done. But Luther insists that we ought to do nothing and undertake nothing at this point except open our ears, listen and believe the Word. "Only this hearing is a hearing of gladness, and this is the only thing we do, through the Holy Spirit, in the matter of justification. So it was a hearing of gladness for the paralytic when Christ said (Matthew 9:2), 'Take heart, My son; your sins are forgiven.' "[9]

2. *Prayer and Hope*

Prayer is the inevitable outgrowth and fruit of justification, of a new and right relationship with God. Realizing that we have no righteousness of our own or anything else with which to plead our cause before God, we accept the precious and costly gift of Christ's righteousness by faith and pray that God will keep us in this grace and complete what he has begun in us "at the day of Jesus Christ" (Philippians 1:6). In this manner Luther interprets the prayer of Psalm 51:11, "Cast me not away from thy face and take not thy Holy Spirit from me." "Look at his great humility," Luther comments on David's prayer, "how anxiously he fears the dangers that threaten those who are justified and have the forgiveness of sins." From this Luther concludes that "both our own experience and examples like this have taught us that no one can ask for grace except one who is justified, and that no one can ask for the gifts of the Spirit except one who is sanctified."[10] The grace of God by which we are justified endows us with the needed strength for prayer and with the spirit of prayer through which we are confirmed in the God-relationship and given the gift of perseverance and the joy of obeying God's good and gracious will.

Our entire hope as believers rests squarely upon Jesus Christ and his justifying grace. Wherever his grace has been received by faith, prayers will be addressed to God. Christ's own words, "If you ask anything in my name, I will do it" (John 14:14), indicate how justification and prayer go hand in hand. From them we learn "that through Christ alone we possess both grace and the granting of

67

prayer, that we first become children of God, entitled to call upon Him, and then also receive what we need for ourselves and others."[11] Through prayer we lay hold of the hope we have in Christ, offering our petitions confidently because we have been declared righteous before God for Jesus' sake and are assured of receiving whatever we ask in the Savior's name.

Our Christian hope is sure because of what God has given us in Christ and because of who Christ is. He is both God and man. The author of the Fourth Gospel, according to Luther, "asserts that Christ is both true man and true God. The factious spirits would be glad to hear Christ make the simple statement that He is either all God or all man." However, Scripture teaches the paradoxical truth about his person. "The word of both, that of God and that of man, is assigned to Christ in the one Person. Holy Writ fuses the two so adroitly that the words sound like those of a true man and, on the other hand, like those of the true and very God."[12]

Justification and prayer are correlative and can be separated from one another as little as the Godhead of Jesus Christ can be severed from his humanity in the one person. It is this inseparability of the two natures, human and divine, that provides an immovable foundation for both the gift of Christ's righteousness which we receive by faith and the spiritual power and hope which are ours through prayer in his name. In his treatise, *Appeal for Prayer Against the Turk*, Luther argues convincingly that the Christians of his day should put their hope neither in their own cleverness nor in their military might. On the other hand, they were not to yield to fear and despair either as if the seen things of life were their only defense. "Our solace, boldness, self-confidence, security, victory, life, joy, our honor and glory are seated up there in person at the right hand of God the Father Almighty.... We commit all to him. He will do all things well as he has from the beginning, does now, and always will do unto all eternity. Amen."[13] For Luther Jesus Christ was, is and will be the Eternal Contemporary of his believing, praying people. Through him they shall gain the victory. That is the Christian hope.

3. *Prayer and Intercession*

Christ is the intercessor for his people before God's throne. When they pray to God in their difficulties, needs, and sufferings, they base them "upon Christ the Mediator. He presents their prayers before God, and they become acceptable and are heard for His sake.

"This is the great honor which belongs to Christians: He has anointed us and made us worthy, so that we may appear before God in prayer." Jesus Christ alone makes it possible for us to pray acceptably to God. Without Christ as our intercessor we are unable to pray rightly in spite of all our impressive efforts and claims. Consequently, unbelievers lack this one essential requirement in prayer. "They do not have this Mediator and High Priest. Everything must have its source in Him. Only through Him does anything avail in the sight of God."[14]

Because Jesus Christ intercedes for us before God, we, too, should intercede for others in prayer in his name and spirit. A Christian dare not restrict his prayers to himself or to the narrow circle of his family or friends. His prayers are to be all-encompassing in their scope, even as Christ was concerned about and prayed for all sorts and conditions of people. "Here every person is admonished to embrace all of Christendom in his heart and to pray for himself and all men, especially for the members of the clergy whose duty it is to administer the Word of God. . . . There is nothing more necessary and profitable for Christendom than this daily bread, that is, that God may grant a well-trained clergy who will preach and make his Word heard throughout the whole world."[15]

The overflowing love of Christ for a world in need motivated his prayers of intercession. A similar love for the great multitude of people in the world should impel us to pray for them. Especially the church in its universality should be the object and concern of our prayers.

> So then true love will prompt us to pray above all else for Christendom, and this accomplishes more than praying just for ourselves. For, as Chrysostom says, all of Christendom prays for him who prays for it. Indeed, in such a prayer he prays together with Christendom for himself. A prayer spoken only in behalf of oneself is not a good prayer. . . . I ask you to note and ponder that it is not without reason that Christ taught us to pray "our Father" and not "my Father," "give us this day our daily bread" and not "my daily bread," that he speaks of "our trespasses," "us," and "our." He wants to hear the throngs and not me or you alone, or

a single isolated Pharisee. Therefore sing with the congregation and you will be swallowed up by the crowd. But if you sing alone you will have your critics.[16]

Luther extols the need and power of intercessory prayer. He calls upon the congregation of Christians assembled in the church as their house of prayer to bring their own needs as well as those of all people before God and to implore his merciful help. Besides, they are to do this out of love for others and with genuine devotion.

"O if any congregation, please God, were to hear mass in this way and pray in this way, so that a common, earnest, heartfelt cry of the whole people were to rise up to God, what immeasurable virtue and help would result from such a prayer!" exclaims Luther. This kind of communal praying would be instrumental in preserving many in their faith and also in converting a multitude of sinners. Its impact would be enormous.

"For indeed, the Christian church on earth has no greater power or work against everything that may oppose it than such common prayer. . . . What matters is not the places or buildings where we assemble, but this unconquerable prayer alone, and our really praying together and offering it to God."[17]

Luther, aware of the many persons and forces that are at work in opposing the kingdom of God in its coming to people on earth, urges his contemporaries to pray fervently for their conversion, providing a model for such praying in his treatise, *A Simple Way to Pray* of 1535. "Therefore, dear Lord, God and Father," he writes, "convert them and defend us. Convert those who have yet to acknowledge thy good will that they with us and we with them may obey thy will and for thy sake gladly, patiently, and joyously bear every evil, cross, and adversity, and thereby acknowledge, test, and experience thy benign, gracious, and perfect will."[18]

In explaining the fourth petition of the Lord's Prayer in the treatise alluded to above Luther advocates intercessory prayer for the ruling authorities, suggesting that one pray for God's blessing in this temporal life, for peace and for protection against war and anarchy. Included in such a prayer would be the various rulers on earth, the emperor, kings, and princes as well as every estate, whether it be a townsman or a farmer.[19]

In another context in the same treatise Luther again takes up the task of providing a kind of model for intercessory prayer. In one prayer he petitions that God may bestow grace and pour his blessing upon home and state, asking that persons may be devout, honor their parents, and obey their superiors. Praying thus for the improvement of the life of the home and of the nation and for the preservation of peace, he sees these petitions as furthering the honor and glory of God, the benefit of those who pray and the prosperity of all.[20]

In both the Small and the Large Catechisms the Reformer interpreted the fourth petition of the Lord's Prayer as not only a request for "everything required to satisfy our bodily needs, such as food and clothing, house and home, fields and flocks, money and property," but also "a pious spouse and good children, trustworthy servants, godly and faithful rulers, good government."[21] In fact he regarded praying for the ruling authorities as having a high priority in our prayer life. Praying for those who rule over us is of such great importance because without stable government and the protection and peace it affords we could not enjoy the continual blessing of having our daily bread and the many benefits which good government confers upon its people.[22]

In his *Lectures on 1 Timothy* Luther makes the candid admission that there was a time in his life when he thought that he would not dare to include in his prayers such important matters as praying for kings. He was reluctant to ask such great things in prayer. However, in time he came to realize that because God is so great and gives such great gifts he actually desires believers to ask for great things. "From the very greatness of the gifts the confidence to ask for great things grows," he concluded. Since God gave his Son, the greatest gift of all, there should be no reluctance on our part in praying for rulers and all those in authority. After all, these are gifts which are inferior to prayer for the remission of sins and eternal life. God, Luther assures us, will therefore give great things to those who ask for them.

Praying for good rulers in his day included for Luther not only the emperor and the princes in Germany but also the kings of France, England and Bohemia, for he considered them all good gifts of God. Yet he held that we must go beyond even this broad scope in praying for the rulers of humankind. Those who do not seem worthy of our prayers for them, our enemies, must likewise be encompassed by our prayers. "The Christian ought to ask for great things and include all men in his prayers." One of the great gifts for which we should pray is peace. To live in peace and quiet is one of God's precious gifts. The gift of peace should therefore be used thankfully and wisely "that we may more quietly be able to discuss the Word, extend the faith, and bring up our children in spiritual, corporal, and moral discipline — in Christian discipline. . . . Let us teach the faith, let us increase the hearing of the Word, let us spread the knowledge of Christ."[23] For that reason prayers of intercession for rulers and all in authority and ultimately for all of humanity, including our enemies and persecutors, are in Luther's teaching so urgent and essential.

The justification of the ungodly is for Luther the burning center of the gospel. Because all of humankind is estranged from God and enslaved to sin by reason of its fallen state the unconditional offer of Christ's righteousness is to be made to all. Those who repent and believe in Jesus Christ as their Savior and Lord have his righteousness imputed to them, putting them into a right relationship with God and marking the beginning of a new life of freedom in the service of God and humanity.

Prayer becomes the dynamic expression of this restored relationship to God. Our forgiveness evokes prayers of thanksgiving and praise to God, and with Christ as the firm, immovable foundation for our lives our Christian hope is certain and unfading. As members of God's kingdom our constant prayer will be that we "may remain faithful and grow daily in it . . . " and "that it may gain recognition and followers among other people and advance with power throughout the world."[24] Only the message of the cross with the justification of the sinner for Christ's sake as its focal point makes it possible for us to believe that God is truly our Father and that we are his redeemed children who can pray to him "with all cheerfulness and confidence."

PRAYER AND THE PRAISE OF GOD

Since God is the Giver of life and salvation it is incumbent upon us as his creatures to give him thanks and praise. In the light of God's good and gracious gifts in both creation and redemption we are by faith impelled to praise him. "You should praise not yourself, but God, in everything good that you have and feel."[25] Justified by grace through faith, we have been set free from our bondage to sin and self and so acknowledge God as the merciful, forgiving, heavenly Father.

Luther's analysis of the human condition in his *Lectures on Romans* was that after the fall of the human race into sin a person is turned in upon himself (*incurvatus in se*).[26] Liberated from this enslavement to self by Christ, our lives, instead of being egocentric, become theocentric. Hence the praise of God is but a logical consequence of having our lives anchored in God. Not to praise and thank him would be a denial of our trust in him. The praise of God in prayer is therefore the direct result of our believing acceptance of his mercy and grace.

No one is exempt from the duty of praising God for all that he has done and continues to do for him. All of us constantly fall short of appropriately praising him, and even if there is someone who is especially pious, he cannot be excused from participating in the praise of God. "Having received a greater measure of grace than others, he can never repay and thank God adequately even for his most insignificant gifts. Indeed, he is unable to praise God sufficiently for his everyday coat or cloak, to say nothing of life, health, honor, possessions, friends, intellect, and innumerable other blessings from God."[27]

The mere fact that God has in his mercy become our God should constitute a powerful incentive for us to praise and thank him. We are undeserving and it is his grace that seeks us out and blesses us with material and spiritual gifts. "We poor mortals have sought so many gods and would have to seek them still if he did not enable us to hear him openly tell us in our own language that he intends to be our God. How could we ever — in all eternity — thank him enough!"[28]

However God may be at work in the world, he is constantly bestowing his gifts upon all people collectively and individually. Aware of God's continuing activity in the world as he renews and preserves his creation, Luther could say: "All this he does out of his pure, fatherly, and divine goodness and mercy, without any merit or worthiness in me. For all of this I am bound to thank, praise, serve, and obey him."[29] In a similar vein he enjoins upon those of us who confess our faith in God a sensitive awareness of his active goodness and preserving and sustaining love. "When we escape distress or danger, we should recognize that this is God's doing. He gives us all these things so that we may sense and see in them his fatherly heart and his boundless love toward us.

Thus our hearts will be warmed and kindled with gratitude toward God and a desire to use all these blessings to his glory and praise."[30]

Particularly in connection with one's participation in the Lord's Supper is the Christian's heart stirred to give thanks and praise to God for his Son's self-giving on the cross for the world's salvation. "Do this in remembrance of me" (1 Corinthians 11:24), said Jesus when he instituted the Sacrament. In the light of this mandate by Christ one should not only think of one's own benefit or need when participating in the Holy Supper, but of the value it has in glorifying God. "But what does it mean to remember him," asks Luther, "other than to praise, listen to, proclaim, laud, thank, and honor the grace and mercy which he has shown us in Christ? Upon this Christ he has directed and concentrated all his glory and worship so that he does not wish to know of any glory or worship apart from Christ, yes, he does not even acknowledge it."[31] This, in Luther's view, is the proper worship of God. Therefore one should never forego such an opportunity. For that reason Luther makes this urgent appeal: "Now if you want to engage in a marvelous, great worship of God and honor Christ's passion rightly, then remember and participate in the sacrament; in it, as you hear, there is a remembrance of him, that is, he is praised and glorified. If you practice or assist in practicing this same remembrance with diligence, then you will assuredly forget about self-chosen forms of worship, for . . . you cannot praise and thank God too often or too much for his grace revealed in Christ."[32] Without the praise of God our praying would be hollow indeed.

But when we are mindful of all his mercies, benefits, and blessings we are moved to praise and thank God for the great love he has shown us in Christ.

Lastly, in the face of death itself, which is an inevitable experience for all members of the human race, we should resort to prayers of praise and thanksgiving. Knowing that God has commanded us to pray and mindful of his promise, we can pray with the confident assurance that he will bestow upon us his strengthening Spirit of hope and comfort. "Therefore, we ought to thank him with a joyful heart for showing us such wonderful, rich, and immeasurable grace and mercy against death, hell, and sin, and to laud and love his grace rather than fearing death so greatly."[33] So with thankfulness in our hearts and with the praise of God on our lips we should be prepared to offer our prayers to God when we are called upon to taste the bitterness of death.

It is evident then that for Luther true prayer always becomes doxological in its content and purpose. By faith God is regarded as the source of the Christian's righteousness, help, hope and strength, and prayer is therefore always directed to God as the fountainhead of unfailing love. Finding refuge and refreshment through his faith in the Lord, the believer cannot but praise and thank him for his many mercies and blessings.

PART THREE

PRAYER AS FRUIT OF THE SPIRIT'S WORK

CHAPTER FIVE

THE EFFICACY
OF PRAYER

To pray aright we need the Holy Spirit. Calling God "Our Father" in faith, as the Lord's Prayer teaches us, is made possible by the Holy Spirit's activity in our hearts. The ability to address God as our Father in prayer is in no sense to be attributed to the innate power of our human nature, but must be traced to the enabling power of the Spirit. On the basis of honest self-examination "we will discover that no man is so perfect as to be able to say truthfully that he has no father here on earth, that he possesses nothing, that he is a total stranger here, and that God is His only Father. For our nature is so base that it always covets something here on earth and will not content itself with God in heaven."[1]

THE HOLY SPIRIT AND PRAYER

The Holy Spirit is responsible for bringing us to faith in God. "Thus the Spirit in and through Christ quickens, sanctifies, and awakens the spirit in us and brings us to the Father, by whom the Spirit is active and life-giving everywhere."[2] Our prayers are the result of the faith kindled in our hearts by the

Holy Spirit. Only as the Spirit keeps renewing and confirming us in this faith can we continue to pray to our heavenly Father as we should.

Luther concedes that the possibility exists of praying in the heart without using words or gestures. Nevertheless, he believes that words and gestures can stir up and kindle the spirit more fully even while "the praying should continue in the heart without interruption. . . . a Christian always has the Spirit of supplication with him, and his heart is continually sending forth sighs and petitions to God, regardless of whether he happens to be eating or drinking or working. For his entire life is devoted to spreading the name of God, His glory, and His kingdom, so that whatever else he may do has to be subordinated to this."[3]

Personal feelings of unworthiness may often act as barriers to our praying. Luther tells us of his being hindered in prayer by such thoughts of unworthiness, causing him to say rather perfunctorily in prayer: "Have mercy on me, O God!" But he goes on to say: "Still the Holy Spirit won out by telling me: 'Whatever you may be, surely you must pray! God wants you to pray and to be heard because of His mercy, not because of your worthiness.' "[4] The mere fact then that we keep on praying is attributable to the work and witness of the Holy Spirit in our hearts. He both enables us to pray and prompts us to continue to do so.

The thought of God's greatness and our own insignificance, flashing on our consciousness at times, may also hinder us in our praying. At such moments we have to overcome this roadblock to prayer. A valiant struggle of the spirit will ensue. How then can one emerge victoriously in this conflict? Luther attributed the victory to the Holy Spirit's strengthening help. "I have learned from my own experience," he relates, "that these thoughts often drove prayer away from me. Nevertheless, by the grace of God I came to the knowledge that I must not surrender to Satan as he attacked me with his arrows, but tearing them from him by the power of the Spirit I turned the weapons against the enemy himself and said: 'You frighten me away from prayer because I am a sinner. But I see that I must pray most of all because of this one reason, that I am a very great sinner and have need of mercy.' "[5]

In the struggle for faith, faith in the mercy and forgiveness of God, the Holy Spirit comes to our aid and makes prayer a strengthening reality. How we picture God in moments of doubts and trials is important. "This picture of a gracious and merciful God is a picture that gives life." Yet we are constantly tempted to picture God on the basis of our own imagination and reasoning. As a result we come up "with the theology of reason, which counsels despair in the midst of sin."[6] We distort the picture of God, falsely believing that it is the right picture. That is why Luther warned repeatedly against constructing a picture of God apart from his own revelation in his Word. It will always be a false picture. But on the basis of our insights and experiences in the world we are so easily led to believe that it is indeed a true picture of God. In order to overcome our human propensity toward a recurring distortion of God's genuine nature and will, we have to turn to the revelation of God in Scripture apart from all reason, philosophy or human wisdom.

The Holy Spirit alone can illumine our minds and convince our hearts and wills so that we get to know and trust in God as he is truly pictured for us in the Bible. He is a God of love, a God of mercy, a God who saves and gives life. "Have mercy on me, O God, according to Thy steadfast love; according to Thy abundant mercy blot out my transgressions" (Psalm 51:1). In his comments on this verse Luther points out that David, aware of God's great displeasure over his fall into sin, implores him to have mercy upon him. His painful consciousness of sin and guilt and his appeal for God's forgiving love are not self-induced. They are based on God's self-disclosure in Scripture. For the Word of God is the basis of the knowledge of who we are before God and what God's attitude toward us is. In the light of the Scriptures "spiritual men learn to distinguish between sinner and sinner, between God and God, and learn to reconcile the wrath of God or the wrathful God with man the sinner."[7]

In the tension between God's wrath and mercy, human sin and divine holiness, the true picture of God as merciful, forgiving, loving, compassionate and caring emerges on the basis of his revealed Word through the Holy Spirit's activity and witness in our hearts. By the Spirit's power through faith in Jesus, crucified and risen for us, we overcome all the false pictures of God that we conjure up by recourse to our own powers of reason and understanding. We are therefore able to reject the picture of a God who imposes unrelenting punishment and who mercilessly grinds out his iron-clad laws in the universe without regard for the misery, heartache, tragedy, suffering, cruelty, exploitation and death of the human race in its checkered history. In Christ the very core and center of God's nature and being is revealed as one of mercy, fogiveness, reconciliation and love.

In the person of Jesus Christ the paradoxical nature of the law-gospel dichotomy is dissolved so that for all who hear and believe the message of the gospel the revelation of God's reconciling love in Christ becomes the manifestation of God's restoring grace and the covering of his wrath against sin. "For only in Christ does the identity of the God as Giver of the law and of the God who in his love has first known us become recognizable and certain. Only Christ could make the voice of the law heard and at the same time silence it."[8] To know God aright, to avoid each and every distortion of his true nature and his will for us as sinful human beings, we have to learn to trust in his self-revelation in Jesus Christ as the one who loved us and gave himself for us, that is, as a God of love. It is only from this innermost and all-controlling picture of self-giving, suffering and conquering love that God is rightly trusted and invoked in our prayers. Without the witness of the Holy Spirit in our hearts neither genuine faith nor acceptable prayer is possible.

To retain faith in this picture of God without distortion requires of believers not only constant vigilance but also continuous struggle, growth in faith, the rooting out of the remnants of sin and the daily renewal of the inner life in God. "The Holy Spirit is given to believers in order to battle against the masks of wisdom in our hearts, which exalt themselves against the righteousness of God; and in order to arouse us to prayer and to the performance of the duties of humanity to all men, especially to the brethren, so that thus both mind and body might be exercised and we might become more holy day by day."[9]

God at times employs the law as an instrument or means to make us aware of our sins, to humble us and to remove our pride in what we can do "so that we learn to live by grace alone and by the kindness of God." When the question is raised as to why God uses the law in this way, Luther's answer is that he wants to preserve us in our monotheistic faith. In other words, he envisions the recurring possibility of a distortion of the biblical picture of God. Referring to Manichaean dualism, he asserts that the Manichaeans "established two principles, of which one was good and the other evil. In good things they ran to the good god, in evil things to the evil god. But God wants us, whether in pleasant or adverse circumstances, to have confidence in Him alone."[10] The Christian faith confesses that God, as a unitary being, has everything under his control in the universe. At this point Luther employs an analogy from nature to make his point. The sun, he says, has not ceased to exist or lost its powerful light and become a dark body because it is temporarily completely hidden from our sight by clouds. The truth is the sun's light is still there, but we are prevented from seeing it. "So God is good, righteous, and merciful even when He strikes. Whoever does not believe this departs from the unity of the faith that God is one, and he imagines another god for himself, who is inconstant, sometimes good and sometimes bad. But it is an outstanding gift of the Holy Spirit to believe that when God sends evil, He is still gracious and merciful."[11]

Only if by the light of the Holy Spirit we continue to put our trust in God in the dark and dreary days of suffering or difficulties or trials, can we also persevere in our prayers and find in the God of all comfort and hope our strength and consolation.

One of the objectives of praying is that by the Spirit's might our hearts might become steadfast in their adherence to the faith that God is forgiving, merciful and gracious. Christ calls him "the Spirit of truth" (John 14:17) who leads us into all truth as our teacher and guide. Such longed-for steadfastness in our clinging to the true revelation of God in Jesus Christ is not easy to maintain. There are many forces at work in the world which seek to engender doubt and disbelief and thus make us incapable of praying with boldness and certainty. Prayer is the weapon we need to use to help us in attaining our goal.

> After we have come to a knowledge of this mercy, we should ask first for this, that this knowledge might remain sure, that our heart might not doubt about the mercy of God nor wander around in all sorts of thoughts which hearts imagine for themselves or which wicked teachings produce. For this gift we need creation and renewal, which takes place through the continuous exercise of spiritual struggles or temptations. . . . We need the certainty of the Spirit, not only be-

87

cause of the devil, but also because of our flesh and the world. They band their troops together, as it were, and want to steal this certainty of doctrine from us.[12]

When David prayed, "Cast me not away from Your face, and take not Your Holy Spirit from me" (Psalm 51:11), he displayed great humility. He was sensitively aware of the spiritual dangers which threaten those who are justified before God and possess the fogiveness of sins. "Without the Holy Spirit he could not pray this. And yet as one who already has the Holy Spirit he prays and sighs this, that he might not be rejected or deserted, that he might not sin again and fall. . . . "[13] Because the prayer, which as an expression of trust in God is pleasing to him, is made by the indwelling power of the Spirit, such a prayer also continues to plead for the Holy Spirit's uninterrupted presence in one's life. Only in this way is the right relationship with God maintained and deepened through continuing prayer, and "daily growth of the heart in the Spirit who sanctifies" the believer, takes place.

The Holy Spirit is present not only in our justification and sanctification, granting forgiveness and making prayer a source of spiritual and moral strength in our lives, but he is also working in us so that we are empowered to confess Christ before the world. It requires constancy to make a fearless confession of one's faith in life. The Apostle Paul, for one, possessed this kind of inner strength in the confession of Christ's name. He could say with a ringing certainty, "Who shall separate us from the love of God?" (Romans 8:35). "It seems to me," observes

Luther, "that in this passage David is asking for the same thing, that he might be able to confess his God freely, despising the dangers of the world."[14]

The inevitable sequence to being justified by God is the confession of his name before others. "This knowledge will not let us be silent, and the world will not let us speak. Therefore we must be confirmed by the Spirit so that we do not fall away from the confession because of dangers."[15] Consequently the prayer for confirmation in our faith by the Spirit arms us with the readiness to risk even our lives in confessing God in the world. By the enabling power of the Holy Spirit we gain the confidence to disregard all dangers and terrors that may arise in the face of such a confession. Luther's autobiographical reference at this point is quite appropriate. He declares,

> Just so, by the grace of God I have also experienced this great gift, that by my teaching and writing I have freely confessed Jesus Christ, my Lord and liberator, against the will of the emperor, pope, princes, kings, and almost the whole world, even amid a thousand dangers to life with which my wrathful enemies and Satan himself were threatening me. So the Lord says to Jeremiah (1:18): "I shall make your face iron so that you do not care who attacks it." And really, the office of teaching in the church requires such a mind that despises all dangers. In general, all the devout should prepare themselves so that they are not afraid of becoming martyrs, that is, confessors or witnesses of God. Christ does not want to hide in the

world, but He wants to be preached, "not between four walls but from the roof" (Matthew 10:27), so that the Gospel shines in the world like a torch on a high mountain or on a watchtower. When this happens, all sorts of dangers are present, and we are really caught, as the German proverb says, between the door and the door jamb. Nor is there anything else that can console us than God's promise that He will not forsake us.[16]

In order that our confession may be steadfast and strong, we ought to humble ourselves in the presence of God and "pray continually for the gift of the Spirit and the increase of faith." While humility will characterize our attitude toward God, we will adopt a courageous and bold posture vis-à-vis the world, fearlessly condemning its errors and sins, even though conflicts, opposition and excommunication may threaten us.

Luther's emphasis on the Holy Spirit's presence and activity in the hearts of believers pervades his writings. He is mindful of the necessity of his presence as the basis for faith in human hearts as well as the constant need of his accompanying witness and power in all the activities of the people of God. Without the active presence of the Spirit the practice of prayer could not be maintained, strengthened and bear fruit. With his help our prayer life will continue to unfold, lead to growth in faith and in godliness and empower us to make the good confession of our faith before others.

The presence and activity of God's Spirit in the Christian life imply that prayer will be the continual accompaniment to whatever one thinks, plans and does. The Spirit's work can be compared with the never-failing supply of pure water gushing forth from a spring refreshing the thirsty soul and empowering it for prayer. Thus the spirit of prayer is always kept alive in the midst of life's activities and happenings.

> Therefore wherever there is a Christian, there is none other than the Holy Spirit, who does nothing but pray without ceasing. Even though one does not move one's lips and form words continuously, one's heart nevertheless does beat incessantly; and, like the pulse and the heart in the body, it beats with sighs such as these: "Oh, dear Father, please let Thy name be hallowed, Thy kingdom come, Thy will be done among us and everyone!" And when blows fall, when temptations thicken, and adversity presses harder, then such sighing prayers become more fervent and also find words. A Christian without prayer is just as impossible as a living person without a pulse. The pulse is never motionless; it moves and beats constantly, whether one is asleep or something else keeps one from being aware of it.[17]

Just as believing and confessing that Jesus is Lord (1 Corinthians 12:3) cannot take place without the Holy Spirit, so genuine prayer is predicated on his dwelling in us. It is the Holy Spirit who helps us in our weakness, interceding for us with sighs too deep for words (Romans 8:26). "Should we not remember, then," asks Luther, "that Paul says that the Holy Spirit helps us in our weakness and cries: 'Abba!

91

Father!"? That is, He emits what seems to us to be some sort of sob and sigh in our heart; but in the sight of God this is a loud cry and a sigh too deep for words." In every situation of need and in moments of weakness we should cling to Christ who gives us the Holy Spirit's help in our prayers. "Then the Father says: 'I do not hear anything in the whole world except this single sigh, which is such a loud cry in My ears that it fills heaven and earth and drowns out all the cries of everything else.' "[18] This is not a long prayer, explains Luther. Nor is it spoken loudly and tearfully. It is merely a sigh. "This is indeed a very short word, but it includes everything. Not the lips but the feelings are speaking here. . . . Therefore the term 'Father,' when spoken meaningfully in the heart, is an eloquence that Demosthenes, Cicero, and the most eloquent men there have ever been in the world cannot attain. For this is a matter that is expressed, not in words but in sighs, which are not articulated in all the words of all the orators; for they are too deep for words."[19]

Not only does the Holy Spirit intercede for us with sighs too deep for words; but he also preaches to us when we are meditating on a specific petition of the Lord's Prayer or on some other word of God so that we are inspired and guided to pray in a more acceptable manner. In this way we learn more from one word from the Holy Spirit's sermon to us than we do from a lengthy prayer of more than one thousand words. Referring to his own way of praying, Luther stated that in praying he did not adhere rigidly to a given pattern. He did not cling slavishly to the exact words of a prayer, but expressed himself in a certain way on one day and in another way on the following day, depending on his personal circumstances. In general, however, he kept before him some basic thoughts and guidelines. On occasion his meditation on one petition of the Lord's Prayer would call forth such a profusion of ideas that he would disregard the other six petitions, "make room for such thoughts, listen in silence, and under no circumstances obstruct them. The Holy Spirit himself preaches here, and one word from his sermon is far better than a thousand of our prayers. Many times I have learned more from one prayer than I might have learned from much reading and speculation."[20]

Luther took seriously the injunction of Psalm 46, "Be still, and know that I am God." He depended upon the power and guidance of the Holy Spirit in his meditations and prayers and showed himself ready in obedient faith to follow God's leading. For us not to do so invites impoverishment of our prayer life and our Christian living. Rigidity and a hide-bound scheme in saying our prayers are therefore to be avoided. This was so important in Luther's teaching on prayer that he recast the advice he had given earlier in connection with meditating on the Lord's Prayer, so that it would be appropriate also when one reflected on the Ten Commandments. He said, "If in the midst of such thoughts the Holy Spirit begins to preach in your heart with rich, enlightening thoughts, honor him by letting go of this written scheme; be still and listen to him who can do better than you can. Remember what he says and note it well and you will behold wondrous things in the law of God. . . . "[21]

The Holy Spirit is our Counselor or Advocate or Helper who, having brought us to faith, continues to support us, strengthening our faith and undergirding us in our prayers. By means of his assistance our prayers become expressions of our trust in God who guides us and helps us to grow in grace, in godliness, and in our faithfulness and obedience to him.

THE CHURCH AND PRAYER

Toward the close of his *Lectures on Genesis* in 1545 Luther, speaking in Latin, enthusiastically interjected in his native tongue, "The church shall be my fortress, my castle, and my chamber. . . . "[22] These words reflect the Reformer's life-long love and sincere concern for the church as the people of God here on earth. One of the simplest and yet most apt definitions of the church from Luther's pen is, "Thank God, a seven-year-old child knows what the church of Jesus Christ is, namely, holy believers and sheep who hear the voice of their Shepherd. So children pray, 'I believe in one holy Christian church.' "[23] It is apparent that Luther thought of the church first and foremost as a community of believers, not as an institution. In it the Holy Spirit is at work. "He first leads us into his holy community, placing us upon the bosom of the church, where he preaches to us and brings us to Christ."[24] The church is thus "a unique community" which "is the mother that begets and bears every Christian through the Word of God."[25] To be a Christian means to be incorporated into the body of Christ, the community of Christians. Only in that body can we be in a right relationship to the head of the church, Jesus Christ. Without Christ as Savior and Lord there can be no church. "For where Christ is not preached, there is no Holy Spirit to create, call, and gather the Christian church, and outside it no one can come to the Lord Christ."[26]

The church is not a building of wood or stone or any other material; it is the people of God or "Christian congregation or assembly" or "a holy Christian people." It is the workmanship of the Holy Spirit, possessing one faith. Even while having a variety of gifts, it is united in love and is without sects or schism. Created by the Word of God, as it is preached and taught in its midst, the church is made to grow, to become strong in its faith, and to bring forth the fruits of the Spirit. When this Christian community assembles for the worship of God, it is principally for the purpose of having the Word of God preached to it and of bringing its prayers of praise and thanksgiving and its petitions to God. Luther emphasized this priority in the clearest terms. He believed "that a Christian congregation should never gather together without the preaching of God's Word and prayer, no matter how briefly. . . . Therefore, when God's Word is not preached, one had better neither sing nor read, or even come together."[27] Assembling for worship, the congregation should hear the Word of God and have it explained. After that it should "unite in giving thanks to God, in praising him, and in praying for the fruits of the Word, etc."[28] It is therefore of primary importance in Luther's view to proclaim the Word of God, to praise, to sing and to pray to God in the congregation at stated times.

The voice of praise and prayer by God's believing people must be heard. In fact Luther regards prayer as a mark of the church. While possession of the holy word of God, the sacraments of Holy Baptism and of the Lord's Supper, the office of the keys, namely, the power to forgive and to retain sins publicly and privately according to God's Word, and the office of the ministry are the five marks of the church that are ranked first, the sixth mark of the church is "prayer, public praise, and thanksgiving to God."[29] Prayer is one of the possessions of God's people by which the Holy Spirit sanctifies them. Fittingly, suffering or the cross is listed as the seventh and final mark of the church by Luther in his treatise *On the Councils and the Church*, so that no one might get the false impression that by prayer the community of Christians escapes suffering, difficulties and persecution in this life. Prayer does not necessarily deliver God's people from all suffering and opposition in the world; but by prayer the church receives strength to stand up to and overcome the sufferings and trials to which it is exposed here on earth.

Th experience of suffering and the cross is applicable to our individual lives as well as to the corporate life of the church. Personal danger, difficulty, sickness, persecution or potential trouble may be removed by God's answer to prayer. But there is also the possibility that in response to our prayers God may instead enable us to bear the particular burden, distress or misfortune that has come our way. In both cases God hears our prayers and answers them according to his grace and infinite wisdom. Because prayer is an act of faith it is heard by God and will not be denied. A believer can be sure of that. "And he actually experiences God's help in every need. Even if he is not immediately delivered from his distress, he knows nonetheless that his prayer is pleasing to God and is heard; and he knows that God enables him to bear and overcome his distress. This ability is tantamount to the removal of the trouble."[30]

Only a few years later in another treatise, entitled *Against Hanswurst*, Luther lists ten marks of the church. In it prayer is regarded as the sixth mark of the church and intercessory prayer as the tenth and final mark. Claiming to have the same prayer as the ancient church, namely the Lord's Prayer, Luther goes on to say, "We have not invented a new or different one; we sing the same psalms and praise and thank God with united heart and voice according to the teaching of Christ, the practice of the apostles and the ancient church, and their command to us to follow their example."[31] In listing prayers of intercession as the tenth mark of the church in this writing Luther is in reality making the claim that the true church does not resort to force or avenge itself but believes in and practices non-violence and love for one's enemies. He asserts that "nobody can deny that we have not shed blood, murdered, hanged, or avenged ourselves in return, as we could often have done and could still do. But as Christ, the apostles, and the ancient church did, we endure, admonish, and pray for others. And, indeed, we do this publicly in church, in the litany and in sermons, just as Christ our Lord did and taught and as the ancient church also did, so that in this we all act according to the ancient practice of the ancient church."[32] Inasmuch as the church is the workshop of the Holy Spirit and his creation in a unique sense, prayers of praise, thanksgiving and intercession mark its pilgrimage through the world.

The common or congregational prayer is particularly prized by Luther. It is all-encompassing in its scope and a source of strength to the believing community. "This common prayer is precious and the most powerful," he declares, "and it is for its sake that we come together. For this reason also the Church is called a House of Prayer, because in it we are as a congregation with one accord to consider our need and the needs of all men, present them before God, and call upon Him for mercy." Prayers of this nature need to be made "with heartfelt emotion and sincerity" and with sympathetic and believing hearts. What sense does it make, asks Luther, if Christians come together for prayer if they do not voice their prayers and petitions unitedly before God, if they "scatter these prayers, and so distribute them that everyone prays for himself, and no one has regard for the other, nor concerns himself for another's need?"[33] The corporate prayer of the worshiping community has therefore special meaning in that it unites the hearts of all in common supplications, praises and thanksgiving to God. Wherever such prayers are brought to God with earnest and heartfelt cries by God's people the benefits and blessings will be of immeasurable value. "For indeed, the Christian church on earth has no greater power or work against everything that may oppose it than such common prayer."[34]

A congregational prayer should moreover bring specific needs and concerns before God. Mentioning these and commending them to God's mercy and good will, we must firmly believe that our prayer is being heard by God. Our neighbor's sin and plight as well as every other need of the whole body of believers on earth should be included in this kind of prayer. "Just as on the cross Christ prayed not for himself alone but rather for us when he said, 'Father, forgive them, for they know not what they do' [Luke 23:34], so we must also pray for one another."[35] Prayer is so important in the church that Luther could say, "But the true church has been founded for the purpose of praying."[36] For that reason Luther also said that the true church is one that prays.[37] It is thereby fulfilling its God-intended function. It has received the first fruits of the Spirit in order that we who belong to it might pray, might put off the flesh, and advance in our sanctification.

Whenever the congregation has assembled for worship and has listened to the reading of the Scriptures and their interpretation, it will then "unite in giving thanks to God, in praising him, and in praying for the fruits of the Word, etc."[38] The church as a community of believers, gathered to hear the Word of God and its message, cannot fail to respond to the address of that same Word by common praise and prayer to God. It will on such occasions also pray the Lord's Prayer which unites Christians in a special way. "The Lord's Prayer binds people to one another," Luther asserted, "that is why it becomes the most powerful prayer."[39]

For Luther the prayer of believers constitutes the right kind of praying. Christ by his work of salvation has made the prayer life of the Christian community what it should be before God. "For prayer is the true work characteristic only of Christians. Before we become Christians and believe, we do not know how to pray or what to pray."[40] Prior to becoming Christians the attempts of persons to pray are vitiated by their reliance upon what they have done or achieved before God. Their hearts, filled with pride, are in doubt as to whether their prayers are heard at all. Their own supposed holiness becomes the basis for dealing with God and praying to him. Instead of being servants of God, they regard themselves as masters and, inverting the order, make God their servant and debtor. Christians, by contrast, rely completely on the grace of God in Christ so that, possessed by and aided by the Spirit, they offer their prayer to God, trusting in the Savior's mercy and the help he has promised them.

Since Christ fulfilled the promises of the Old Testament by his death on the cross and his resurrection, he has instituted "a new divine worship." Because of this he wants us "to distinguish between the Old and the New Testament, between His forerunners and His advent and present reign."[41] While the patriarchs and prophets prayed in the right spirit of faith during the days of the old covenant, relying on the Christ whom God had promised and who was to come, now that he has come true prayer must be based on belief in him and his completed work of redemption. God has fully revealed himself in Jesus Christ. Consequently, prayer in Christ's name is the only acceptable and completely reliable way of praying to God with believing hearts and with full confidence that God hears such a prayer in our common worship.

If God answered the prayers of the patriarchs Moses, Joshua and Elijah and all other Old Testament believers, surely he must answer our prayers because we have the same word and Spirit of God when we pray to him. "We are members of his church, which is the bride of his beloved Son. He cannot ignore the church when it earnestly beseeches him."[42] It is for the sake of the church as the people of God that the Lord preserves the world and continues to shower his gifts and blessings upon all who dwell upon the earth. Our prayers as a Christian people will be answered by God, provided we pray with repentant, believing hearts and in a fervent spirit of commitment to his kingdom. "For whatever God gives to the entire world, to heathen and to the Turks, to good and bad, he gives it all through and for the sake of his dear children, that is, the Christians who fear him, who know themselves to be sinners, who willingly accept his punishment and heartily trust in him, who pray and call on him in every time of trouble."[43]

The church is the place where the triune God is at work, bringing to faith and sanctifying his people through the forgiveness of sins and his many gifts. It is the Holy Spirit who carries out the redeeming and sanctifying purpose of God among his people and kindles and strengthens their faith. "The church exists where the word of God concerning such a faith is rightly preached and confessed."[44] Therefore it behooves us as his own to ponder what the Holy Spirit accomplishes in the church, to be thankful that we have been called and incorporated into the church, to confess our lack of faith and gratitude, and to pray for a strong and steadfast faith through which we shall inherit the promised kingdom of righteousness and eternal life.

The Word of God as the means of grace by which the church is constituted through the working of the Holy Spirit also calls for and commands the observance of the two sacraments of baptism and the Lord's Supper. "Baptism is nothing else than the Word of God in water, commanded by the institution of Christ," says Luther.[45] It is the word joined to the water that makes baptism a spiritual power which grants forgiveness of sin. Moreover, infants too should be baptized because they are included in the promise of the redemption which Christ has wrought by his cross and resurrection. They, too, are born again by water and the word and belong to Christ's body, the church. Connected with the rite of baptism are the prayers of the believing community which witnesses this event and with becoming earnestness prays for their incorporation into the body of Christ. In his *Order of Baptism* of 1523 Luther calls attention to the importance of having all believers witnessing a specific baptism join in intercessory prayer for the child that is being baptized.

> For here, in the words of these prayers, you hear how meekly and earnestly the Christian church concerns itself about the little child and how it confesses before God in plain undoubting words that he is possessed by the devil and is a child of wrath, and prays very diligently for aid and grace through baptism that he may become a child of God. . . .

Remember, too, that it is very necessary to aid the poor child with all your heart and strong faith, earnestly to intercede for him that God, in accordance with this prayer, would not only free him from the power of the devil, but also strengthen him, so that he may nobly resist the devil in life and death. And I suspect that people turn out so badly after baptism because our concern for them has been so cold and careless; we, at their baptism, interceded for them without zeal.[46]

It is the unavoidable and serious responsibility of the community of believers to be present at the administration of a baptism or baptisms, to listen to God's word, and to join in prayer for the one or the ones to be baptized. All sponsors and all persons present are to participate in the intercessory prayers spoken by the officiating minister with fitting reverence and genuine devotion because by this baptismal act the baptized "become children of life, heirs of all the gifts of God, God's own children. . . . "[47]

Luther's composition of the so-called "flood prayer" which he substituted for a traditional collect in the *Order of Baptism* is eloquent proof of his deep concern for fervent intercessory prayers on behalf of the person to be baptized. In his teaching and understanding of baptism the heartfelt prayers of the congregation supply and surround the baptismal candidate with the spiritual ambience consistent with the saving power of Christ's word that is addressed to the baptized and creates faith in the human heart.[48]

Similarly, the observance of the Holy Supper of our Lord as Christ's gift to his people for the strengthening of their faith on their pilgrimage through life cannot take place in an appropriate way if it is not celebrated in connection with a joyful confession of faith and the offering of prayers of thanksgiving and praise to God.

> When this faith is rightly present the heart must be made glad by the testament. The heart must grow warm and melt in the love of God. Then praise and thanksgiving will follow with a pure heart, from which the mass is called *eucharistia* in Greek, that is, thanksgiving. We praise God and give him thanks for his comforting, rich, blessed testament, just as a man is thankful and grateful and glad when a good friend has presented him with a thousand or more gulden.[49]

Luther sees two principal results from receiving the Lord's Supper with believing hearts. First of all, our reception of the body and blood of Christ, together with the bread and the wine, as a sure pledge of divine forgiveness and favor moves us to offer prayers of thanksgiving and praise to God. Second, through it we are comforted and granted grace. "These two ways cannot be bad or constitute an abuse, but must be good and pleasing to God. For we cannot deal with God in more than two ways, namely, by giving thanks and by voicing our petitions." By thanking God for the gift of his grace in the sacrament we acknowledge his goodness and honor his name. By bringing our petitions to him we glorify him as the source of future blessings. Such an act of faith in prayer Luther calls bringing to God "the sacrifice of praise and the sacrifice of prayer,"[50] stating that no one can do more or render to God greater honor. Indeed, as a result of our believing participation in the Holy Supper, we are motivated to keep on thanking God and praying to him and thus are induced to receive the sacrament again and again thankfully in faith.[51] In the church as the community of believers therefore the Holy Spirit continues to create, renew, deepen and strengthen faith through the proclaimed Word of God and the continuing administration of the sacraments so that the praise of God and prayers in Jesus' name never cease.

CHAPTER SIX

THE PURPOSE AND PRACTICE OF PRAYER

How can we come to know God's will for our lives through prayer? Is it not simply a matter of praying in faith for what we desire and then confidently expecting God to give us what we have prayed for? This is not necessarily the case. The Apostle Paul makes the observation that "we do not know how to pray" (Romans 8:26). Our personal wishes expressed in prayer are not always in conformity with God's will. Sometimes spiritual trials assail us in order that we might through them be made aware of God's will for us and so be prepared to accept what God wants us to have.

GOD'S WILL AND OUR PRAYERS

1. *Spiritual Trials and Prayer*

"It is not a bad sign but a very good one," explains Luther, "if things seem to turn out contrary to our requests. Just as it is not a good sign if everything turns out favorable for our requests."[1] The reason for this is that God's counsel and will are by far superior to our limited perceptions and plans. This conclusion is confirmed for Luther by the words from Isaiah

55:8-9: "For my thoughts are not your thoughts, neither are your ways my ways, says the Lord. For as the heavens are higher than the earth, so are my ways higher than your ways, and my thoughts than your thoughts."

God may bestow upon us what we have prayed for in a way that it appears to be contrary to what we had asked. Yes, God may be offended by what we have asked in prayer, causing him to do even less for us in response to our prayers. However, God does this for a purpose "because it is the nature of God first to destroy and tear down whatever is in us before He gives us His good things. . . . "[2]

Such spiritual trials (*Anfechtungen*) actually render us capable of receiving his gifts and works. We are ready to receive God's counsels and works only after we have ceased making our own plans, have let our hands rest and have become purely passive before God, outwardly by the cessation from works and inwardly by the surrender of our desires. "Therefore, when everything appears to be hopeless for us and all things begin to go against our prayers and desires, then those unutterable groans begin. And then 'the Spirit helps us in our weakness' (Romans 8:26). For unless the Spirit were helping, it would be impossible for us to bear this action by which He hears us and accomplishes what we pray for."[3]

No one escapes the trials of life. By recourse to prayer we can entreat God for help in the midst of them. In this connection Luther relates from Jerome's *Lives of the Hermits* how a young hermit who desired to get rid of his unwholesome thoughts was

107

told by his older companion, "Dear brother, you cannot prevent the birds from flying over your head, but you can certainly keep them from building a nest in your hair."[4] Our prayers for divine assistance can help us in overcoming the temptations which assail us.

The purpose of such trials is that we might get to know ourselves as persons who are weak and easily tempted to sin, to go to God in prayer and to depend on his grace by which we can overcome them. Trials keep us alert, train us in humility and patience and make us acceptable to God as his children.[5] We also learn to acknowledge that God's will is at all times best for us so that we cherish and desire it for ourselves.[6]

It is not difficult for us to say, "I believe in Christ"; but it requires struggle and effort to maintain such a faith firmly in our hearts. To this end the Holy Spirit is granted us in order that we might pray and by God's grace win the victory amid life's trials.[7] After we have overcome these temptations, " . . . there is nothing left for us to do for God but to thank Him. Whatever we are, live, and have is a gift of God. . . . "[8] His Spirit confirms us in our faith so that we might give him the praise and glory for his help.

God may delay the answer to our prayers. He may even not give us everything for which we have asked. However, he gives us everything for our improvement. When he chastens us with the rod of affliction and we cry out to him in prayer, he does not stop at once. "He likes to hear our crying and sighing. It is the mark of pious children who mend their ways and do not run from Him but want to remain good children."[9]

Whenever we pray to God in time of trial or distress, we should not try to prescribe the ways, means or time for his answer. Luther regarded that as tempting God. For that reason "we should not determine the when and where and why, or the ways and means and manner in which God should answer our prayer. Rather, we must in all humility bring our petition before him who will certainly do the right thing in accordance with his unsearchable and divine wisdom."[10]

The dangers and trials in life are designed to incite us to prayer because God wants to help us. Consequently we should humbly prostrate ourselves before him and bring to him our prayers. His promise of help gives us the assurance that in his time and in his way he will deliver us for our good and to his glory.[11]

Boldly Luther applied the parable of the importunate widow and the unjust judge to God's attitude toward us when we pray to him in times of trouble and distress. God seems to be hiding from us. Apparently he does not let himself be found. Yet he knows of our needs and circumstances and will come to our aid in response to our prayers in his good time. Luther was convinced that often prayers are answered by God the moment the first syllable has been uttered because he is our gracious Father who wants to help us in our distress.[12]

God is sovereign. He is going to have his way and will in ordering the world's future course in accordance with his purpose. As Christians we pray that his will might be done, as we put our trust in his grace and guidance. "As God's name must be hallowed and his kingdom come even without our prayer, so must his will be done and prevail even though the devil and all his host storm and rage furiously against it in their attempt utterly to exterminate the Gospel. But for our own sake we must pray that his will may be done among us without hindrance, in spite of their fury, so that they may accomplish nothing and we remain steadfast in the face of all violence and persecution, submitting to the will of God."[13] In the midst of our trials and difficulties then we bring our prayers to God, trusting in his fatherly compassion and help as well as his gracious and good will toward us for Jesus' sake.

2. *The Theology of the Cross and Prayer*

Luther's theology of the cross, drawn from the Bible, makes the daring assertion that it is precisely in the dark moments of life, in suffering, sorrow and helplessness that trust in God is created and strengthened. Thus conformity to Christ as his disciples becomes a reality in our lives by the power of the Holy Spirit. This mysterious way of God's dealing with us is indicated to us by the prophetic words that God "does a strange work in order to perform his own work" (Isaiah 28:11).

> People, therefore, who do not have the Spirit, run away from God's working and do not want to let it happen to them, but they want to shape themselves and their own lives. But people who have the Spirit are helped by him. Hence, they do not despair but they remain confident when they feel that the opposite of what they have sincerely prayed

for happens. For God's working must be
hidden and we cannot understand its way.
For it is concealed so that it appears to be
contrary to what our minds can grasp.[14]

It is important to note the close connection between the presence and work of the Spirit and the
believer's prayers. While we as a rule understand our
own projected work before it is done, it is not possible
for us to comprehend God's work until it has been
completed. God proceeds with his work much like an
artist who comes upon some material that can be
suitably molded into a work of art. The suitability of
the material is, as it were, an unfelt prayer for the
form which the artist has in mind and goes on to
fashion in conformity with its appropriateness. In a
similar way God, aware of our feelings and thoughts
and what we are praying for, what we are fit for, and
what we long for, comes to us, grants us our prayers
and begins to mold the form of art he has in mind for
us. As a result the form and model we had designed
come to nought and everything seems to turn out in
opposition to our ideas "when the Spirit comes over
us and is about to do what we pray."[15] In reality,
however, God is carrying out his saving power and
plan in our lives by fashioning us in the likeness of
his Son.

God certainly hears our prayers even though "we
do not know what to pray for" (Romans 8:26). However, instead of asking him for something great, we
are too weak and impotent to make large requests. In
response to our praying God first nullifies our insignificant petitions for which we prayed in our weakness and instead gives what the Spirit asks for us.

111

We must learn to pray in the name of Christ. His disciples at first prayed in their own name, that is, according to the flesh. Later they would pray in Jesus' name and so in the power of the Spirit according to the divine will. "For," concludes Luther, "he prays in the name of Christ who prays also in sufferings."[16]

The proof that we do not know what to pray for is that we do not accept the good which God offers us. In our weakness we become fearful and want to run away from what God has to give us. But the Spirit prays for us and helps us in our infirmity. Even though we preach that God's power, wisdom, goodness, righteousness and mercy are great and marvelous, we do not really understand them. We try to comprehend them metaphysically, that is, "as things that are apparent and not hidden, although He has hidden His power under nothing but weakness, His wisdom under foolishness, His goodness under severity, His righteousness under sins, and His mercy under wrath.... We ask for salvation, and He, to save us, increases our damnation and hides His answer under this kind of thunder."[17] Consequently God is with us in all the weaknesses and sufferings, the fears and frustrations of life in a hidden way so that our trust and our prayers are ultimately vindicated by the Holy Spirit's help and intercession.

Our conformity to Christ takes shape in the midst of the sufferings of this present age as we address our prayers to God. Luther therefore offers these comforting and reassuring words to all believers who want to be well prepared to face death:

In Christ he [God] offers you the image of life, of grace, and salvation so that you may not be horrified by the images of sin, death, and hell. Furthermore, he lays your sin, your death, and your hell on his dearest Son, vanquishes them, and renders them harmless for you. In addition, he lets the trials of sin, death, and hell that come to you also assail his Son and teaches you how to prepare yourself in the midst of these and how to make them harmless and bearable. And to relieve you of all doubt, he grants you a sure sign, namely, the holy sacraments. He commands his angels, all saints, all creatures to join him in watching over you, to be concerned about your soul, and to receive it. He commands you to ask for this and to be assured of fulfillment. What more can or should he do?[18]

Our prayers are thus the divinely commanded expressions of faith by which we let God deal with us in accordance with his saving word and will revealed in Jesus Christ and sealed by the help, strength and comfort of the Holy Spirit. Besides, because Christ was humbled and exalted more than all the saints in the history of humankind we should not deem it strange or odd if we, too, have to endure suffering and affliction in our lives.[19] It is the way in which we are conformed to the image of Jesus Christ.

The cross of Christ has revealed to us a God of love and comfort, the kind of God who has regard for and loves the contrite, the vexed and the troubled. The will of God is that we should have life, not death, for he is a God of salvation, not of damnation, a lover and helper of the humble and the damned. The Holy Spirit must teach our hearts this spiritual wisdom lest we be crushed by bitterness and sadness and do not even dare to pray. Therefore we should sing the song, "The sacrifice of God is a troubled spirit" (Psalm 51:17), believing that our trouble and affliction please God, all the while trusting in him alone.[20]

"We have to learn," Luther reminds us, "that a Christian should walk in the midst of death, in the remorse and trembling of his conscience, in the midst of the devil's teeth and hell, and yet should keep the Word of grace, so that in such trembling we say, 'Thou, O Lord, dost look on me with favor.' "[21]

Each one of us is called upon to bear a cross and afflictions without being crushed by our sorrows and without falling into despair. We would rob God of his divinity if we should fail to continue to trust in his mercy. Like cowardly soldiers, we may be tempted to desert the colors in the face of the first feeling of temptation; but as disciples of Jesus we should press on because we have not yet obtained the prize and are not already perfect (Philippians 3:12). Only the Holy Spirit who commends to us this humility and contriteness of heart can help us win the victory.[22]

3. Doctrinal Integrity and Prayer

Luther confesses that God's word is all-powerful. At the same time he is acutely aware of the existence of many words of God. In fact, God's words are as diverse as our human ailments and needs. Some persons have to feel the accusing power of God's word, others its comforting and uplifting strength. While God has indeed entrusted his word to us as his people, he does not want us to manipulate or falsify it. We should therefore accept it, bow humbly beneath its truth and power and pray that the right words of God will be spoken to us and that we will listen and believe them.

In prayer we utter our petition to God that his word may address us and help us in our particular situation. "But since the proper choice of the words of God, as also their effectiveness, does not rest with men but solely with God, we ought to ask God that he himself might select the holy words for us and that they be given us either directly by him or by another human being."[23]

Above everything else God wants to have "his Word taught in its purity and cherished and treasured."[24] Prayer must somehow be connected with preaching and teaching the Word of God in its truth. For that reason Luther suggests this kind of prayer for our spiritual bread, which is the Word of God, "O heavenly Father, since no one likes your will and since we are too weak to have our will and our old Adam mortified, we pray that you will feed us, strengthen and comfort us with your holy Word, and grant us your grace that the heavenly bread, Jesus Christ, may be preached and heard in all the world, that we may know it in our hearts, and so that all harmful, heretical, erroneous, and human doctrine may cease and only your Word, which is truly our living bread, be distributed."[25]

It is by the activity of the Holy Spirit that God's Word becomes efficacious in human hearts. For that reason Luther combines Word and Spirit in his prayer to God. "So we pray that thy kingdom may prevail among us through the Word and the power of the

Holy Spirit, that the devil's kingdom may be overthrown and he may have no right or power over us. . . . "[26] To this end we need to persevere in our prayers so that God might help us to remain steadfast in our faith in his Word.

Preaching the Word of God is pivotal and important; but this divinely ordained function must be accompanied by prayer. After charging his disciples in the Sermon on the Mount with the mandate of preaching the Word and of living Christian lives in accordance with it, Jesus, observes Luther, added "an admonition to prayer. By this he intends to teach them that, second only to the office of preaching, prayer is the chief work of a Christian and an inseparable part of the sermon. He also wants to indicate that because of all the temptations and hindrances we face, nothing is more necessary in Christendom than continual and unceasing prayer that God would give His grace and His Spirit to make the doctrine powerful and efficacious among us and among others."[27] Prayer for the efficacy of the preached Word includes the petition for the gift of the Holy Spirit by whose presence the Word accomplishes its renewing and saving work in human hearts.

In the Reformer's view there are two priestly offices which should be faithfully discharged in a Christian congregation. The one is the office of teaching, which occurs when a sermon is preached or when absolution is granted to penitent, believing hearts. The other is the office of praying for oneself and others, which usually takes place after the sermon. "For a prayer should follow every sermon. A good Our Father should follow a good sermon. For one should pray for the increase of faith that we may grow in the blessing, lest the devil take it from us."[28] Neither one of these two primary functions in the church, teaching and praying, dare be neglected. The first one is so important because through it we hear God speaking to us. We thus get to know of his grace and will for us. The second function, or office, inevitably follows the first because we speak in prayer to God who hears us. "Through the administration of the sacraments, God descends and speaks with me," states Luther. "There I hear. On the other hand, I ascend and speak into the ears of God, who hears my prayer."[29]

By prayer we are confirmed in our faith. Yet such praying should always take place in close connection with reflection on the Word of God. "This is another good thing about prayer. If you use it and practice it and thus ponder the Word of His promise, your heart keeps getting stronger and firmer in its confidence, and finally gets much more than it would have otherwise."[30]

In order that our preaching and teaching of God's Word might remain sound and pure without any admixture of error or without being distorted, we need to resort to prayer. In answer to prayer God grants us his Holy Spirit, enabling us both to believe his Word and to preserve it in its purity. Justified before God through faith in his mercy shown us by Christ, we know that we cannot obtain God's favor by anything we might have or do. It is solely because God is merciful to us that we are in a right relationship with him. According to Luther the prophetic writer of Psalm 51 moves from the teaching of believing in a merciful God to enjoining prayer, "as if he were to say: 'Thus far I have shown the method of justification, the manner of true repentance and of the forgiveness of sins. Now nothing is left but that we should pray that this knowledge might be broadcast and practiced among all the people. There will be no lack of false teachers who teach the Law and their sacrifices in such a way that this part of the teaching about the free mercy of God is completely neglected. Therefore prayer is necessary to keep sound doctrine among the people against such men.' "[31]

Luther advocated prayer as the necessary spiritual weapon with which to oppose false teachings and to undergird the efficacy of all preaching and teaching of the Word of God. "But here we learn in what way heretics are to be resisted: They are indeed to be opposed by the external Word; but unless passionate prayer is added to it, it will hardly achieve much. Prayer is responsible for the fact that our preaching, teaching, and writing accomplishes something."[32]

Keeping the message of the gospel unadulterated requires vigilance and prayer. Doctrinal integrity is not to be viewed as the result of intellectualistic efforts in and by themselves; it is rather a spiritual undertaking that is aided and strengthened by prayer. "But to the external Word one must join prayer by which the devil is very hard pressed and driven into the corner. Prayer curbed Arius, Mani, Sabellius; it crushed the Pharisees and the unbelieving synagogue; it has overcome the originators of many impious beliefs in our age. . . . "[33]

One cannot vanquish heretics by means of disputations because they are not persuaded by human arguments. God's Word must win the victory.[34] However, the practice of prayer in connection with the preaching and teaching of the Word of God dare not be overlooked or forgotten. Prayer is a critically important and much needed spiritual undertaking by which the teaching of God's Word in its truth, purity and efficaciousness in the Christian community can, by the Holy Spirit's gracious operation, be preserved and furthered. "For that reason it is necessary that we also combine prayer with sound doctrine for the purpose of extinguishing the flaming darts of the evil one. . . . "[35]

4. *Sanctification and Prayer*

Luther distinguishes between two kinds of righteousness. The first is an alien righteousness which is granted us by Christ through faith in his name. By the gift of this righteousness we are justified by grace through faith. "Through faith in Christ, therefore, Christ's righteousness becomes our righteousness, and all that he has becomes ours; rather, he himself becomes ours. . . . This is an infinite righteousness, and one that swallows up all sins in a moment, for it is impossible that sin should exist in Christ."[36]

The second kind of righteousness is our righteousness which results from and is effected on the basis of the alien righteousness. Luther speaks of it as occupying itself with good works, crucifying the desires of the sinful self, and expressing itself in love toward one's neighbor. Of it he says,

> This righteousness follows the example of Christ in this respect [1 Peter 2:2] and is transformed into his likeness (2 Corinthians

119

3:18). It is precisely this that Christ requires. Just as he himself did all things for us, not seeking his own good but ours only — and in this he was most obedient to God the Father — so he desires that we also should set the same example for our neighbors.[37]

With the second kind of righteousness Luther has in mind the Christian's sanctification, which is indeed to be sharply distinguished from the alien righteousness imputed to a person by faith, but which is nonetheless indissolubly connected with the latter. In our life on earth our own righteousness or sanctification is fragmentary, incomplete. Having its inception in us through baptism and faith, it grows and becomes greater; but it will not find its fulfillment here on earth. We must continually pray for growth in grace so that this proper righteousness of ours might increase and establish itself more fully in our personal lives.

And so we are partly and not wholly righteous. Hence we have sin and debt. Therefore, whenever we pray that righteousness be perfected in us and our sin taken away, we ask at the same time for the end of this life. For in this life the proneness toward evil is not perfectly healed (just as, to speak figuratively, the Children of Israel were unable to drive out the Jebusites). This is the reason why the prayer "Hallowed be thy name" (Matthew 6:9) (and this happens when our nature is hallowed from evils and sins) is immediately followed by the petition: "Thy

Kingdom come" (Matthew 6:10), which is as much as to say that it will be fully hallowed only in thy Kingdom. But also this Kingdom will come only through tribulations. This is why there then follows the petition: "Thy will be done" (Matthew 6:10), as Christ prayed in the Garden at the time of his tribulation. . . . [38]

The sanctification of our lives is the work of the Holy Spirit in a special sense. In response to our prayers he comes to our aid, forgiving us our sins daily and renewing our strength in our fight with sin and evil. "Now we are only halfway pure and holy. The Holy Spirit must continue to work in us through the Word, daily granting forgiveness until we attain to that life where there will be no more forgiveness. In that life are only perfectly pure and holy people, full of goodness and righteousness, completely freed from sin, death, and all evil, living in new, immortal, and glorified bodies."[39]

Sanctification is conceived by Luther as an ongoing process. In explaining the petition "Thy kingdom come" in his *Personal Prayer Book*, he expresses in the form of a prayer the dynamic drive toward holiness in the lives of believers. "Grant that your kingdom, begun is us, may daily increase and improve, lest cunning malice and apathy for doing good overcome us so that we slip back. Rather grant us both earnestly to resolve and to be able to make a beginning to live a pious life as well as to make vigorous progress in it and reach its goal."[40]

Pride rears its ugly head so easily in our Christian lives. Praying that God's name may be hallowed, we seek to eradicate the sin of pride which is the root and fountainhead of all sin. "Now you observe," comments Luther, "that this petition contends against this accursed arrogance, which is the head and the life and the essence of all sins. Just as no virtue can have its being and be accounted good when tainted with this arrogance, so no sin can live or harm when this arrogance is dead. . . . Hence, since no one is without pride, and since everyone covets his own name and honor, there can be no one for whom this petition is not very necessary and useful."[41]

Where pride is dethroned and unbelief overcome the plant of faith can take root and grow in the human heart. In contradistinction from the scholastic notion of grace as a quality infused into the heart, Luther upholds the biblical teaching "that grace is the continuous and perpetual operation or action through which we are grasped and moved by the Spirit of God so that we do not disbelieve His promises and that we think and do whatever is favorable and pleasing to God. . . . Just as life is never idle, but as long as it is present, it is doing something — for even in sleep life is not idle, but either the body is growing, as in children, or other works of life are felt in breathing and the pulse — so the Holy Spirit is never idle in the pious, but is always doing something that pertains to the Kingdom of God."[42] This constant striving to please God has to be attributed to the working of the Holy Spirit in our hearts. Because the Spirit's operation in our lives is of the utmost importance we dare not fail, above all else, to pray for spiritual gifts, like faith, God's Word, and the Holy Spirit who helps us in bearing our sorrows, leads us to do God's will, preserves us from error, and grants us a blessed departure from this earthly life.

It is particularly in our specific vocations in life that we can serve our neighbor and please God. In this way our daily works become genuine expressions of our prayer life and glorify God's name. "There is a saying ascribed to St. Jerome that everything a believer does is prayer and a proverb, 'He who works faithfully prays twice.' This can be said because a believer fears and honors God in his work and remembers the commandment not to wrong anyone, or to try to steal, defraud, or cheat. Such thoughts and such faith undoubtedly transform his work into prayer and a sacrifice of praise."[43]

Because prayer leads to action so that our works are in a sense the incarnation of our prayers Luther rightly poses the rhetorical question, "If no other work were commanded, would not prayer alone suffice to exercise a man's whole life in faith?"[44] Possessing a living faith, one will pray without ceasing. This means that even while one is busily engaged in one's work one can still speak with God in the heart. Such spiritual praying is therefore the continual accompaniment to our labors, making both what we pray and what we do by faith acceptable in God's sight. In this way prayer becomes work and work in turn a fulfilled prayer. Throughout our lives we exercise our faith by praying, seeking to attain an ever greater correspondence between our prayers and our works.

The struggle in prayer has to continue. We might be tempted to think that "the habit of true prayer" is not so important. As a result we can become lazy or careless, lax and listless with regard to praying. God's word must rouse us to engage in prayer constantly, so that we can carry out the responsibilities of our several callings in life for the purpose of serving our neighbor in love and so doing God's will.

The persistent peril that threatens our growth in grace, according to Luther, is our failure to value above everything else the Word of God with its rich provisions of mercy and truth. We tend to take God's word for granted. This is the case because our hearts are "harder than an anvil and, like rocky soil, keep the root of the Word without sap and fruit."[45] Is there any way in which we can deal effectively with such obdurateness and complacency? Luther proposes prayer as the appropriate spiritual resource for contending against this dangerous attitude. He confesses candidly, "I myself feel in me this hardness of heart, and I hate it and also offer prayers against it every day."[46] His own awareness of not responding joyfully and gratefully to the abundant availability of God's word induced him to pray daily for a heart that was open and receptive to the message of God's redeeming and renewing grace in Christ. Prayer as the believing response to the word of God keeps us vigilant so that we are properly prepared to receive the proffered help and to live more and more in accordance with God's will.

It is clear then that the teaching of God's word ought never to be divorced from its implementation in our lives. Closing the gap between what we teach and what we practice as Christians was a matter of serious concern for Luther. "It is not enough for us to have the Word and to know and understand everything we should — both the doctrine of faith and about comfort and victory in every trouble. Something more is required and that is action, in order that subsequently we may live as doctrine and knowledge teach and guide us."[47] The goal should always be to make practice conform to teaching and exhortation. Realizing this objective is most difficult because of the conflict between our old nature, the flesh, and our new creation in Christ, the life in the spirit. In this struggle Luther advised that we raise our eyes heavenward and pray to the heavenly Father so that we might be given the necessary strength to overcome the hindrances of the flesh. It will then be our experience that by ourselves we can do nothing, but that "both the beginning and the end, the willing and the doing" must be sought in prayer and granted by God as a gift of his grace.[48]

The prayer of Psalm 51, "Cast me not away from thy face, and take not thy Holy Spirit from me," is interpreted by Luther to mean a genuine longing for holiness of life. "I apply this to sanctification of the flesh and to mortification, or the new obedience which ought to follow in the justified, that a married man lives chastely with his wife and amicably with his neighbors and that a magistrate does his duty diligently in administering the commonwealth and is not indulgent toward the sins of his subjects."[49]

The sum and substance of our sanctification is contained in the prayer, "Let thy good Spirit lead me on a level path" (Psalm 143:10). "The good Spirit is the Holy Spirit," says Luther. "He creates gentle, kind, and good hearts, which walk the right path, on which they seek God in all things and not themselves."[50] Ultimately, God by his word and Spirit will prevail. His kingdom will come. To this end we should pray that the gospel might be proclaimed throughout the world, that the kingdom of darkness might be utterly destroyed, that God's kingdom might be fully established at the end of the world, "and that we may live forever in perfect righteousness and blessedness."[51] Then the goal of our sanctification, begun on earth and prayed for faithfully, will have been reached.

THE POWER OF PRAYER AND THE COMING OF THE KINGDOM

Luther both believed in and experienced the power of prayer. In the first place, according to him, this power is predicated on the omnipotence of God. Compared with God's almighty power the strength of all the peoples on earth is as nothing. In the second place, God does not permit his name permanently to suffer disgrace on earth. The sin of dishonoring his name will not go unpunished. So when we honor God's name and invoke it in our prayers and others defame us for doing so, they are in reality opposing God and dishonoring his name which we are revering by faith and prayer. "Is it not God Almighty Himself and His name? Do you not see the gun being loaded? Since God will not suffer His name to be blasphemed, and we still pray and ask that it be hallowed and honored, don't you believe that this prayer will discharge the gun? And the bullet?" Luther raises these questions in his comments on Psalm 118:1-4, and then proceeds to assert that God will vindicate his name and glory, even as he has done in the history of peoples in the past. This vindication, when it takes place, will cause consternation among worldly and ecclesiastical leaders. Moreover, the German people themselves had better beware because they will not escape God's righteous judgments either. "Perhaps it will be the Turk or some other sentence or plague of God, bringing death and destruction," Luther points out. At any rate, we can be certain tht God will devise ways and means to vindicate his name and his righteousness, as human history itself demonstrates. "This means that we Christians crush the heathen through our prayers, while God actually does it for the sake of His name, which we use and honor."[52]

By praying that God's name might be hallowed on earth we are aligning ourselves with his almighty purpose which he is carrying out. God is at work in the universe and his power must be reckoned with in our prayers. So sure is Luther of the beneficial effects of these prayers that are brought to God by his believing people that he concludes, "Thus it is certain that whatever still stands and endures, whether it is in the spiritual or in the secular realm, is being preserved through prayer."[53]

The answer to prayer depends in no small measure on a spirit of concord and unanimity among Christian people. By faith we live in a right relationship with God. On the basis of our trust in God through Christ we are bound to live a life of love toward our neighbor. Such a posture entails avoiding everything that may injure or offend members of the Christian community. We should always be forgiving toward one another, knowing that we cannot be forgiven either whenever we fail to forgive others. "Where anger and ill will are an obstacle, this spoils the whole prayer and prevents one from being able to pray or to wish any of the preceding petitions either.. .. When we plan to come before God in prayer for what we are to obtain, we must not be disunited or divided into schisms, factions, and sects, but we must be tolerant toward one another in love and remain of one mind."[54] Having the same faith and being united in one spirit, we will offer prayers that will manifest a powerful and salutary influence in our midst and in the world.

We may be proceeding quite satisfactorily in our faith and life as Christians. Yet we should know that there are all sorts of transgressions and offenses that seek to hinder our progress in Christian living. We battle against these foes of faith "continually with all our might, but the strongest shield we have is prayer. If we do not use that, it is impossible for us to hold our own and to go on being Christians."[55] While there are many obstacles to living the Christian life on earth, neglect of prayer means surrendering the weapon we need most of all. Jesus' admonition, "Ask, and it will be given you; seek, and you will find; knock, and it will be opened to you" (Matthew 7:7), needs therefore to be heeded. We cannot keep on being Christians in deed and in truth without tapping the resources of spiritual power through unceasing prayer.

Three formidable hindrances to Christian living confront us. They are the triumvirate of our own flesh, the world and the devil. "There, you see, are three troubles that press us down hard and will not

128

get off our neck as long as we have life and breath. Hence we have continual reason for prayer and invocation."[56] King Hezekiah faced overwhelming odds when Jerusalem was besieged by the great army of Sennacherib. Humanly speaking his situation was hopeless. But he commended his cause to God in prayer and the Lord answered him and freed him from his foe. Consequently prayer "is a very precious medicine, one that certainly helps and never fails, if you will only use it."[57]

Christ wants his disciples to be keenly aware of their own insufficiency in the face of distress and weakness. Besides, they will find themselves in situations when they experience trouble, want, opposition and perplexity. This happens in their lives in order that they might remain humble and conscious of their helplessness. "Then they will exercise their faith all the more by prayer and petition, and will experience His power in weakness and in suffering the more surely, because they will be impelled to call upon Him and implore Him."[58] The result of such believing prayer will be twofold: First, their hearts will be made sure that they have a compassionate God. Second, God will empower them to help others through their prayers. In this connection Luther makes the astounding assertion that Christ's disciples, reconciled to God and with all their personal needs met, become gods themselves and saviors of others by virtue of their supplications. Having become children of God, they will mediate between God and their neighbors, will serve them, and assist them in becoming followers of Christ and heirs of the kingdom of God. The knowledge of Christ is such a great delight and treasure for his disciples that they regard it as a privilege to step forth boldly in sharing this knowledge with others through teaching, exhortation, prayer, praise and confession. Their longing and prayer are that others too may become believers in Christ. In this way the power of prayer is demonstrated.

Praying diligently and earnestly is an important work in our Christian lives because of the many beneficial consequences. Next to preaching the gospel, through which God addresses us personally and offers us his grace and good gifts, "the greatest and foremost work we can do is to speak to Him in turn through prayer and to receive what He gives us."[59] The need for prayer is so great because through prayer we keep what we have and secure God's defense against our enemies. Prayer proves to be the power by which we obtain comfort, strength and help in our lives and protection against as well as victory over those who oppose us.[60]

In his Table Talk Luther relates how on a certain occasion his wife Catherine became gravely ill. In the face of this seemingly hopeless situation, he resorted to prayer and later reported, "I begged God to let my Katie live, and, restoring her, he gave her a good year on top of it all."[61]

On another occasion, when Melanchthon, exhausted and depressed over the bigamy of Landgrave Philip of Hesse, fell prey to a serious sickness in the city of Weimar in June of 1540, Luther boldly prayed for his recovery and literally snatched his ill colleague from the jaws of death. His prayer was answered. He reported, "In that instance our Lord

God had to listen to me, for I threw the whole burden at his feet and kept dinning into his ears all his promises which I was able to enumerate from Scripture, insisting that he had to answer my prayer if indeed I were to trust his promises."[62]

In the year 1537 Luther experienced an unexpectedly severe attack from gallstones at Smalcald where he and his colleagues had gathered to consider theological issues while the princes were discussing their political strategy as members of the Smalcald League. His illness became so serious that his recovery seemed doubtful. Miraculously, however, he regained his health, attributing his restoration to the intercessory prayer of concerned believers in local congregations.[63]

In his appeal for prayer against a threatened invasion by the Turks in his day he designated the earnest prayers of Christians as their chief means of help and hope. "If we have done our part," he counseled, "and have armed ourselves with weapons of prayer, we may say with Joab, 'Be of good courage' [2 Samuel 10:12]."[64]

In his commentary on the petition "Thy kingdom come," Luther articulates a prayer in which he entreats God to convert the enemies of Christian people. "Dear Lord, God and Father," he writes, "convert them and defend us. Convert those who are still to become children and members of Thy kingdom so that they with us and we with them may serve thee in thy kingdom in true faith and unfeigned love and that from thy kingdom which has begun, we may enter into thy eternal kingdom."[65]

131

The eschatological fulfillment of Christ's promises is the necessary precondition for the fullness of joy which the Savior promised to all who believe in him. Christians experience heartache and sorrow as they observe how God's name is being desecrated and his gospel disregarded. They also know that at times they themselves are opposed to the spirit of joy Christ promised to give them. The progress of God's kingdom on earth seems so slow to them that they begin to sink into the mire of despondency and are weighed down with sadness. Their joy is kept from being perfect.

"Therefore," exhorts Luther, "prayer for help and strength must be added, in order that our joy may finally become pure, complete, and perfect. You must not seek this help and strength in yourself or in the world; for that kind of joy is impure, and in the end death will sweep every bit of it away."[66] Christ himself calls upon his followers to continue to pray confidently for the joy that will be full, "as will surely be the case eternally after this life."[67] In this sense, the power of prayer has an eschatological thrust in that it enables us to wait in hope for the complete establishment of God's kingdom in the life to come, and with it fullness of joy.

Luther's buoyant trust in God and his word of promise in Christ continually surfaced in a faithful and fruitful practice of prayer. As a fitting testimony to this kind of commitment to prayer we have the statement of his personal secretary Veit Dietrich. In 1530 Luther remained secluded at the Castle Coburg in southern Saxony while the Diet of Augsburg, convened by Emperor Charles V, was taking place some one-hundred-fifty miles away. During those tense and uncertain days the destiny of the Reformation movement appeared to be hanging in the balance. From the Coburg Dietrich reported about Luther, "I cannot admire his extraordinary steadfastness, joy, faith, and hope enough in these miserable times; but he nourishes them constantly by zealously busying himself with the Word of God. No day passes by without him spending at least three hours in prayer, hours which would seem best suited for studying. . . . That is why I do not doubt that his prayers will have great influence on this practically lost cause of the Diet. . . . "[68]

Justus Jonas, Luther's colleague and friend who attended the Diet at Augsburg and participated in the theological discussions there, concurred completely with Dietrich's assessment concerning the effectual power of Luther's prayers. After the public reading of the Augsburg Confession at the diet on 25 June 1530, Jonas sensed how precarious the fate and future of the reform movement within the church was. Writing to Luther, he implored him to pray without ceasing. "For," he told him, "we behold and with our hands almost touch the fruit and effect of your prayer and the presence of your spirit."[69]

Luther's own historical judgment confirms these observations made by his contemporaries. "Thus at the Diet of Augsburg," he recalled a year or so later, "the devil was trying to devour us. The situation was so desperate and intense that the whole world expected violence to break out, as some spiteful people had been threatening." An open rupture of the prevailing peace could easily have occurred. "But, through our prayers God came to our aid . . . ,"

Luther concluded gratefully. "He gave us a good peace and a year of grace, the likes of which there have not been for a long time, better than we could have hoped for."[70]

Perhaps there is no clearer testimony to Luther's high estimate of the importance and power of prayer in the church on earth than this brief statement of his:

> No one would believe that the power and efficacy of our prayer is so great if we did not speak from experience. But it is a great thing when someone becomes aware of the circumstances of a need and of the enormous need itself and then can proceed to pray. This I know that as often as I have prayed in earnest and it was a real concern for me, my prayers were certainly answered in a richer measure and I received more than I desired. To be sure, our Lord God at times delayed his answer somewhat, but he answered me nonetheless.[71]

A PROPHETIC REAPPRAISAL OF PRAYER

Luther's rediscovery of the gospel, occasioned by his ardent search and study of the Scriptures, deeply affected both the theological meaning and the practice of prayer. His being captive to the Word of God with its liberating message of redemption in Christ resulted in the prophetic reappraisal of prayer for both the church as a community of believers and the individual Christian. The impact his reassessment of Christian prayer had was pervasive and profound. "Luther's vigorous, healthy, and cheerful type of devotion to prayer . . . is the most important contribution made to the subject in the entire history of Christian prayer."[1] This scholarly estimate of Luther's role in redefining and practicing prayer has to be taken seriously. From what has been said about the nature and purpose of prayer in the context of Luther's theology it is obvious that basic biblical insights and principles determined how he understood prayer and practiced it.

In his *Preface to the Wittenberg Edition of Luther's German Writings* of 1539, which he composed in preparation for the planned edition of his German works, Luther proposed what he believed to be "a correct way of studying theology." He had gleaned this procedure from his own perusal of Psalm 119. "There," he said, "you will find three rules, amply presented throughout the whole Psalm. They are *Oratio, Meditatio, Tentatio*," that is, prayer, meditation and spiritual trial (*Anfechtung*).[2] On the basis of his journey of faith and his own personal experience he found these three components of spirituality to be vital, necessary and effective in a faithful appropriation of the Christian heritage.

As is to be expected, he gives first place to the Bible, which is the source of true knowledge and wisdom and "which turns the wisdom of all other books into foolishness, because not one teaches about eternal life except this one alone."[3] A prayerful approach to God's Word is therefore essential. For that reason Luther advises that one kneel down in one's room "and pray to God with real humility and earnestness," asking for the enlightenment of the Holy Spirit so that one may rightly understand the message of Scripture.[4] This way of beginning one's study of the Word is essential inasmuch as the Scriptures are not subject to one's own rational powers of understanding and insight. The Holy Spirit has to guide a person in the proper discernment of the truth and meaning of God's Word.

In the second place, meditation on Scripture, which follows prayer, involves diligent attention to the meaning of various words in their context and a prayerful reflection on the message conveyed. This meditative process is an undertaking which makes it possible for a person to strengthen his faith and to appropriate the riches of God's grace and truth revealed in his Word. Adhering faithfully to the external Word of Scripture is a precondition for the inner enlightenment of heart and mind by the Holy Spirit.[5]

Finally, spiritual trials are the ways and means by which the knowledge and understanding one has gained from meditating on Scripture are put to the test in the struggles of daily living. As a consequence one will experience "how true, how sweet, how lovely, how mighty, how comforting God's Word is, wisdom beyond all wisdom."[6] Such testing of one's faith in the encounter with various persons and events in the multitudinous settings of life is never an easy matter. Trust in God, and his word will be subjected to all kinds of stresses and strains. The world will respond with opposition, misunderstanding and enmity. Doubts and misgivings will seek to demolish the citadel of faith. But one's eventual triumph over unbelief is assured, as one reverts to prayer and meditation on God's word and gives God the glory and praise for his grace.

In Luther's view preparation for prayer is both possible and meaningful; but there is never anything meritorious involved in getting ready to pray. Reading and meditating on God's Word are means to which we ought to resort in making such preparations. However, the novel element, recaptured by Luther in the Reformation, is that all our preparations for prayer lack each and every claim to merit or

137

worthiness before God. In the depth of our lostness and despair we can plead only God's undeserved mercy and forgiving grace in Christ.[7]

Regardless of the posture we may assume in prayer — kneeling, standing, sitting, with upraised or folded hands — Luther's chief concern is that our prayers should be genuine expressions of faith, articulating the heart's constant sighing and humble begging before God. And because prayer calls for the exercise of our faith, we have to fight against laziness and apathy. Neglect of prayer is a constant temptation to which we may succumb. So we should conquer our sluggish nature and come regularly before the Lord in prayer. For that reason Luther's summons to prayer in his exposition of Psalm 118 is both appropriate and needful.

> You must learn to call. Do not sit by yourself or lie on a couch, hanging and shaking your head. Do not destroy yourself with your own thoughts by worrying. Do not strive and struggle to free yourself, and do not brood on your wretchedness, suffering, and misery. Say to yourself: "Come on, you lazy bum; down on your knees, and lift your eyes and hands toward heaven!" Read a psalm or the Our Father, call on God, and tearfully lay your troubles before him. . . . Here you learn that praying, reciting your troubles, and lifting up your hands are sacrifices most pleasing to God. It is His desire and will that you lay your troubles before Him. He does not want you to multiply your troubles by burdening and torturing yourself. He wants you

to be too weak to bear and overcome such troubles; He wants you to grow strong in Him. By His strength He is glorified in you.[8]

Our commitment to prayer and our valiant wrestling with God in prayer are vital expressions of faith, leading to experiences by which we become "real Christians. Otherwise, men are mere babblers, who prate about faith and Spirit but are ignorant of what it is all about or of what they themselves are saying."[9]

THE THEOCENTRIC PERSPECTIVE

The theocentric nature of both faith and prayer in Luther's theology is discernible throughout his writings.[10] This underlying theocentricity[11] is given forceful expression in his many expositions of and references to the Lord's Prayer in which we leave the matter of what God will give us and what is beneficial for us in God's hands. Luther believes that the Lord's Prayer establishes the right order in our praying. In the first three petitions of this prayer Christ has specified three goals, the hallowing of God's name, the coming of his kingdom and the doing of his will, which must always take precedence over the four petitions which follow.

Since our trust is in God and his forgiveness, love and care we can confidently leave everything in his almighty hand. "Preference must be given to God's name and His kingdom; if this is done," Luther infers, "then our interests will surely follow."[12] The sovereignty of God in his created world combined with the revelation of his saving love in Christ and his cross are expressed in the Lord's Prayer in such a way that God is and remains the ultimate source and center of all that we need, hope and desire in our lives.

Because the Lord's Prayer is the epitome and model of all prayers its theocentric character was both recognized and valued by Luther. "The Our Father is my prayer," he said. "I pray it and on occasion add something from the psalms. . . . In short, of all prayers there is nothing like the Our Father; I pray it in preference to any psalm."[13] In Luther's estimate it is the most consummate prayer in existence, "the loftiest and noblest prayer under the sun"[14] and therefore a reliable guide and goal in all praying.[15]

In his *Commentary on the Sermon on the Mount* Luther deals briefly with the Lord's Prayer, calling it "the very best prayer that ever came to earth or that anyone could ever have thought up."[16] Again he underscores the theocentric nature of the prayer Christ taught his disciples by calling attention to the fact that the first three petitions are designed to give God "the glory that is due Him." When therefore we pray these petitions from the heart we are exalting God and his rule above everything else in the world. "Thus we acknowledge that He is supreme in all three of these areas, but that the others are his instruments by which He acts to accomplish these things."[17] Our human instrumentality in God's rule and plan makes the theocentric nature of faith and prayer evident.

From this theocentric perspective it becomes possible for us to acknowledge gratefully that "God does not always do what we desire but what is beneficial for us." In his wisdom and love he bestows his blessings upon us. However, we do not always ask for what is truly good for us and others, but what seems good to us. In such instances God answers our prayers by not doing for us what we are asking. "That is why," says Luther, "we pray in the Lord's Prayer for the hallowing of God's name, for the coming of his kingdom, and for the doing of his will before we pray for our own concerns and well-being in life. In these matters God undoubtedly does, not what seems good to us, but what is truly good."[18]

If God would always grant the petitions we bring to him in prayer, he would be our prisoner and his sovereign wisdom, power and love could not be realized in our lives. Hence, even though our prayers are heard, they are answered in accordance with the will of God, "which is better than ours."[19]

In all this the Lord's Prayer retains its unrivaled excellence and value because it is "the best form of a prayer" which has been prescribed for us by Christ himself. Since he knew human need in all of its complexity and diversity, the words of the prayer he taught encompass the entire gamut of what we as his people ought to pray for. While this does not exclude both the possibility and advisability of expressing our own particular desires and needs in other words, we can be completely certain that our praying the Lord's Prayer pleases God and is heard by him.[20]

As a kind of summation of his lifelong practice of praying the Lord's Prayer and his frequent comments on it the mature Luther left us this eloquent testimony of its deep spiritual meaning and importance for him:

> To this day I suckle at the Lord's Prayer like a child, and as an old man eat and drink from it and never get my fill. It is the very best prayer, even better than the psalter,

141

which is so very dear to me. It is surely evident that a real master composed and taught it. What a great pity that the prayer of such a master is prattled and chattered so irreverently all over the world! How many pray the Lord's Prayer several thousand times in the course of a year, and if they were to keep on doing so for a thousand years they would not have tasted nor prayed one iota, one dot, of it! In a word, the Lord's Prayer is the greatest martyr on earth (as are the name and word of God). Everybody tortures and abuses it; few take comfort and joy in its proper use.[21]

PREVAILING UPON GOD IN PRAYER

Precisely because Luther looked at prayer from the theocentric point of view he was able to speak of it as possessing great power and efficacy in the life of the believer and the church. Preaching the gospel, through which God speaks to us and offers us his help and blessings, has primary importance in the church and must therefore claim our highest allegiance. But next to it prayer is "the greatest and foremost work," by which we speak to God and receive "comfort, strength, and well-being for us ourselves as well as our defense against, and our victory over, all our enemies."[22]

God hears us when we pray, but he does not always give us what we are asking for without delay. He wants to be entreated. He desires that we persevere in our prayers with fervor and earnestness. "Even though this praying is cold at the outset and does not immediately obtain help, yet we should know that help is postponed in order that prayer may become perfect and stronger. For there is wonderful power and omnipotence in prayer,"[23] declares Luther. The Christian is able to invest prayer with unlimited might on account of the theocentricity of his faith which, guided and controlled by God's saving will, relies on him and his almighty power in carrying out his promise of salvation.

The Reformer had learned the undeniable truth of this stupendous claim concerning the power of prayer in the school of experience during the tumultuous events that took place when the Reformation of the church was in progress. He therefore set forth his convictions about the potent force of prayer from the vantage point of his later years as a reformer in a famous letter to Melanchthon in April of 1540. "But whatever aspect matters may assume, we can achieve all through prayer which alone is the almighty queen of human destiny," he reminded his colleague at Wittenberg. "Through it we guide what has been decided, correct past mistakes, put up with what cannot be changed, overcome what is evil, preserve what is good, even as we have done till now; and we have experienced the power of prayer of which the papists know nothing. . . . "[24] Upholding the theocentric nature of the gospel — it makes known God's saving deed in Christ — and committed to giving God the glory for his redeeming love, he could rightly attribute omnipotence to the prayers that were brought to God in humility and faith.

In speaking of the unconquerable power of prayer Luther even goes so far as to claim that God will change his plan and intention in response to a believer's prayer. It is a matter of biblical record, he points out, "that God does the will of those who fear Him and subordinates His will to ours, provided we continue to fear Him." He did this very thing for Lot who, in the face of the imminent destruction of Sodom and Gomorrah, was directed to flee to the hills to save himself and his family. Lot, however, prayed that he might be permitted to flee to the small city of Zoar instead, and God granted him his petition. "Thus this account serves to rouse and spur us to prayer in all our dangers, since God wants to do what we want, provided that we humbly prostrate ourselves before Him and pray. . . . And in Scripture there are more evidences of this kind; they prove that God allows Himself to be prevailed upon and subordinates His will to ours."[25]

Such remarkable instances in answer to our prayers have to be construed in the light of God's ordered and revealed will in his Word, for God has bound himself to what he has promised in it and he will therefore do it. On the other hand, Christian prayer makes no reference or appeal to God's hidden or secret will outside of his Word of promise.

"Who then can comprehend the lofty dignity of the Christian?" asks Luther in his treatise *The Freedom of a Christian*, only to answer, "By virtue of his royal power he rules over all things, death, life, and sin, and through his priestly glory is omnipotent with God because God does the things which he asks and desires, as it is written, 'He does the will of those who fear him and hears their prayer.' "[26] So awesome is the power of believing prayer according to Luther that we can alter God's will and actually change the course of human events. "Thus I fully believe," he observed in his *Lectures on Genesis*, "that if we devote ourselves to prayer earnestly and fervently, we shall prevail upon God to make the Last Day come."[27] When this happens, however, God's absolute rule is not abridged. God continues to be God, but within his plan and purpose there is an elasticity according to which, on certain occasions, he answers our importunate prayers even while he keeps on pursuing his will and way. Even in such instances the mystery of God's activity and rule remain impenetrable for us.

Luther was convinced that prayer could effect miracles of healing. He experienced them personally when he came desperately ill at Smalcald in 1537, when his wife Catherine lay on her sickbed and was near death's door and when Melanchthon was in such poor health that his demise seemed imminent. In all three instances God had been prevailed upon in prayer to restore them.[28] But these miracles of recovery from illness were in Luther's view by far inferior to the miracles of the new birth in baptism, God's gracious gift in the Lord's Supper, the bestowal of forgiveness in the absolution and the resulting liberation from sin, death and eternal damnation. He held that believers should therefore not value miracles of bodily healing too highly, making faith depend on their occurrence.[29] He himself was once present at the bedside of a woman who became critically ill in childbirth. Deeply moved by her plight, he comforted her and confidently prayed with her for her restoration. However, in this case God did not let himself be prevailed upon. The woman died. Luther, bowing humbly beneath the divine disposal of events in this situation, nonetheless believed that God had heard his prayer in a way that this devout woman would thank him for it in the life to come.[30]

THE PRINCIPLE OF INHERENCE

Because God has spoken and continues to speak to us in his Word, we in turn believingly address him in our prayers. He is the God who speaks (*deus loquens*). He speaks to us and we respond in trust with words of thanksgiving, adoration, praise and petition. Prayer inheres in God's word because the word is spoken to call forth faith and the response of prayer in human hearts. A house of worship, according to Luther, has but one purpose, "that nothing else may ever happen in it except that our dear Lord himself may speak to us through his holy Word and we respond to him through prayer and praise."[31] Prayer is the expression of a living faith in God's word of promise. Therefore the divine promise and human prayer belong together. God's word is the dynamic, creative power by which faith is born in the human heart. This faith, knowing itself to be in a right relationship with God, spontaneously engages in spiritual prayer to God without audible words, but it does not stop there. Spiritual prayer will inevitably result in vocal or outwardly audible prayer as a manifestation of its vital relationship to God. Outward prayer can never precede inward prayer. If it does, it is a hypocritical prayer that hides the lack of faith. For that reason the spoken words of a prayer are not in themselves a sign of real faith. Luther always insisted on the priority of faith, on making a tree good so that it might bear good fruit.[32] It is however impossible to separate genuine prayer from faith in the heart because such faith is bound to express itself in appropriate ways before God and confess the truth before the world.

Our faith in God's word entails bringing our prayers to God and making known whose we are and whom we serve. This inseparable connection between the word of God, faith, prayer and confession establishes the principle of inherence as a vital and meaningful part of Luther's teaching on prayer. Prayer as the chief manifestation of our faith in God's word gives evidence of our not having accepted God's grace in vain. If, as Luther once said, "every spiritual trial is a sign of a loving God," [33] faith, which takes hold of the promise of his word, exercises itself in prayer which seeks God's mercy and strength to overcome these trials and gain the victory.

PRAYER AND CHRISTIAN UNITY

Luther readily acknowledged the reality of the church's existence in the various church bodies of his day. Even though he engaged in sharp polemical attacks against the Church of Rome throughout his career as a reformer, he freely conceded that there were true Christians in that communion. His willingness to make such a statement was based on the evidence that certain criteria or marks of the church were present in it. Holy baptism, for example, as the sacrament of God's prevenient grace, was faithfully practiced in it. Thus the baptized were made children of God and incorporated into the body of Christ, the church. The Word of God, too, in the text of the holy Gospel, was still read from the pulpit in everyone's language, making it possible for believers to be nurtured and strengthened in their faith.

Further marks of the church's existence were the bestowal of the forgiveness of sin through the absolution by the priest both publicly to a congregation and privately to individuals in the confessional. The Holy Communion was also given to the faithful, though in a somewhat truncated form by withholding the cup form the laity. The holy ministry as the office for preaching and caring for souls continued its service to the people by those who were ordained to the priesthood. Last of all, the practice of prayer by its use of the psalter, the Lord's Prayer, the Creed and the Ten Commandments was upheld. Besides, good Christian hymns and canticles supplemented the devotional treasure used for praying. The possession of all these scripturally approved practices made it certain for Luther that the church as a communion of saints was to be found in the church of Rome. "For they are all the ordinances and fruits of Christ with the exception of the robbery of the one form [of the Lord's Supper]. For that reason Christ has surely been here among his own with his holy Spirit and has preserved the Christian faith in them."[34]

It is noteworthy that among the marks of the church mentioned above Luther included prayer. It is however, not prayer in general, but Christian prayer as based upon and guided by the psalter, the Lord's Prayer, the Creed and the Ten Commandments. It is particularly the Lord's Prayer with its specific content that makes Christian prayer deeply meaningful. That is why Luther once remarked about the Lord's Prayer, "What we do mean to say is that all other prayers that do not understand and express the content and meaning of this one are untrustworthy. The psalms, to be sure, are also good prayers, but although they fully embrace the main points of this prayer, they do not express them as clearly."[35] In this sense the doctrinal content of the Lord's Prayer contains the reliable teaching of God's word by which true prayer is gauged and offered to God. The Lord's Prayer as *the* Christian prayer given to believers by Christ himself binds them all together, even as baptism as the rite of entry into the church is for all the baptized the one common foundation for faith and prayer in Jesus' name. Luther's frank acknowledgement that there were true Christians in the Roman Church prompted him to regard the common use of the Lord's Prayer as a unifying factor in the face of their separate existence in an ecclesiastical organization.

In a similar way the Reformer was cognizant of sharing certain basic teachings with sister churches of the Reformation. In his sharp disagreement with Zwingli and his followers over the doctrine of the Lord's Supper, Luther documented his agreement with them in the Marburg Articles by noting their common adherence to fourteen articles of the faith. However, in the fifteenth and last article, he confessed that, although there existed a consensus about the use of both bread and wine in the Supper according to Christ's institution of it, about a spiritual partaking of the Lord's body and blood and about its purpose of exciting to and strengthening faith, no agreement was reached about the real presence of Christ's body and blood in the Sacrament. Because Zwingli and his party did not subscribe to the doctrine of the real presence Luther advocated that "each side should show Christian love to the other side insofar as conscience will permit, and both sides should diligently pray to Almighty God that through his Spirit he might confirm us in the right understanding."[36]

Here, too, prayer was enjoined by Luther as the way in which there might eventuate a true and mutually acceptable interpretation of the Lord's Supper as a basis for Christian unity. In the face of existing conditions in the church of his day the Reformer revealed how he longed for unity and how greatly he relied on prayer in preserving the purity of the gospel as the source of unity and continuity in the church. "The situation," he contended, "requires fervent prayer and great concern, that a purer doctrine may be handed down to posterity."[37]

For Luther the primary and indispensable possession of the church is the eternal word of God as the source, basis and guide for the faith and prayer of God's people. It is *the* norm (*norma normans, non normata*) by which all the church's beliefs and traditions, teachings and practices are to be tested. At the center of it is the gospel of God's forgiving and restoring love in Christ as "the true treasure of the church." The faith and prayers of Christians, deriving from this gospel, bear witness to its redeeming and unifying power.

Praying for the unity of God's people became an unavoidable obligation for Luther in the face of the divisions that were plaguing the one, holy, catholic church (*una sancta catholica ecclesia*) of his age. Nowhere does he give expression to his fervent longing for the unity of the church more warmly and sincerely in prayer than in the last stanza of that short hymn, "Lord, Keep Us Steadfast in Thy Word," which, next to "A Mighty Fortress Is Our God," is perhaps the most widely used of all his hymns.

> God Holy Ghost, who comfort art,
> Give to thy folk on earth one heart;
> Stand by us breathing our last breath,
> Lead us to life straight out of death.[38]

Our prayers are the sacrifice of our hearts and lips, offered to God in faith and accepted by him for the sake of Jesus Christ our Lord. "Our sacrifice of prayer is valid before God only if it is included in the sacrifice of Christ. As prayer in Jesus' name it can, so to speak, never be severed from Christ's priestly sacrifice."[39] Nor can prayer be divorced from the Word and its unifying power. "For whoever believes the Word of the apostles, he is given the assurance on account of Christ and on the strength of this prayer [in John 17] that he shall be one body and loaf with all of Christendom, that what is beneficial or hurtful to him as one member of it shall also have been beneficial or hurtful to the entire body and that not only one or two saints but all the prophets, martyrs, apostles, all Christians, both those on earth and those with God, suffer and are victorious with him, fight for him, help him, protect and rescue him."[40] Because Christian prayer unites us in the church as the body of Christ on the basis of the Savior's high-priestly prayer and sacrifice on the cross for us, a joyous exchange between us all as its members takes place, so that we bear the deficiencies, sufferings and hardships of one another as well as share all blessings, comfort and joy. Prayer, understood in this inclusive sense, is a precious and powerful resource for all Christian people.

Luther was in no sense indulging in hyperbole when he spoke of the incalculable power of prayer. By faith he himself had experienced its marvelous might and beneficial blessing. In the light of God's revealed Word, the Bible, he therefore assigned to prayer the high priority and profound significance it has in Christ's church on earth, summing it all up in these weighty words:

> Now it is necessary above all to know for certain that we have the Word. For this is the foundation and basis of our assurance that we are hearers and that God is speaking with us. Concerning this no one should be in doubt; for he who does not know it, or doubts, will surely mumble prayers with the vain repetition customary among hypocrites. But he is unable to pray.

> However, where this foundation, which is the Word of God, has been laid, there prayer is the ultimate help. No, it is not help; it is our power and victory in every trial.[41]

ABBREVIATIONS

BC   *The Book of Concord.* Translated by Theodore G. Tappert, Jaroslav Pelikan, Robert H. Fischer and Arthur C. Piepkorn. Philadelphia, 1959.

Bek.   *Die Bekenntnisschriften der evangelisch-lutherischen Kirche*, 2nd ed. Goettingen, 1952.

CR   *Corpus Reformatorum.* Halle, 1834 ff.

LCC   *The Library of Christian Classics.* Volume XV. *Luther: Lectures on Romans.* Philadelphia, 1961.

LW   *Luther's Works. American Edition.* Edited by Jaroslav Pelikan and Helmut T. Lehmann. St. Louis and Philadelphia, 1955 ff.

WA   *Luthers Werke. Kritische Gesamtausgabe. [Schriften].* Weimar, 1883 ff.

WABr   *Luthers Werke. Kritische Gesamtausgabe. Briefwechsel.* Weimar, 1930 ff.

WATR   *Luthers Werke. Kritische Gesamtausgabe. Tischreden.* Weimar, 1912-1921.

WML   *Works of Martin Luther.* Philadelphia, 1915 ff.

NOTES

Introduction

1. Alfred Tennyson, *The Poetic and Dramatic Works of Alfred Lord Tennyson* (Boston & New York, 1898), p. 67.
2. Friedrich Heiler, *Prayer A Study in the History of the Psychology of Religion* (New York, 1932), pp. xiii and iv.
3. *Ibid.*, p. 1. As a student of comparative religions Heiler failed to note the unique character of Christian prayer in the light of God's revelation in Christ in contrast with the contents and practice of prayer in other world religions.

Chapter 1. The Need For Prayer

1. Willem Jan Kooiman, *Luther and the Bible* (Philadelphia, 1961), p. 10.
2. *WA* 3, 125. 33-34 (*LW* 10, 121).
3. *WA* 3, 422.18-21 (*LW* 10, 359).
4. *WA* 3, 446.29-32 (*LW* 10, 391).
5. *WA* 3, 448.38-40 (*LW* 10, 394).
6. *WA* 4, 146.15-24 (*LW* 11, 295).
7. *WA* 4, 375.22-26 (*LW* 11, 511).
8. *WA* 56, 466. 6-10 (*LW* 25, 458).
9. *WA* 56, 466.15-23 (*LW* 25, 459).
10. *WA* 56, 467.9-10 (*LW* 25, 459).
11. *WA* 56, 467.26-27 (*LCC* XV, 349); see page 2 of this chapter.
12. *WA* 56, 468.4-6 (*LW* 25, 460).

13. *WA* 56, 468.7-8 (*LW* 25, 460).

14. *WA* 56, 468.14-16 (*LW* 25, 460).

15. *WA* 56, 469.3-12 (*LW* 25, 461). Frederick the Wise was the ruler of Electoral Saxony and Luther's sovereign who had initiated considerable building operations for church and monastery from 1513 to 1514 and who was responsible for the many foundation masses in All Saint's Church.

16. Rudolf Damerau, *Luthers Gebetslehre bis 1515* Erster Teil in *Studien zu den Grundlagen der Reformation*, Vol. 12 (Marburg 1975), p. 225.

17. *WA* 6, 562.8-14 (*LW* 36, 109). Basic teachings of both scholasticism and mysticism were repudiated by Luther with increasing clarity and candor from 1513 to 1520, during which time he lectured on the Psalms and various New Testament books (Romans, Galatians and Hebrews). At the same time some of the insights of the mystics helped him in developing his biblical theol-ogy. See Otto Scheel, *Taulers Mystik und Luthers reformatorische Entdeckung* (pp. 298-318), in *Festgabe fuer D. Dr. Julius Kaftan* (Tuebingen, 1920); Rudolf Damerau, *Die Demut in der Theologie Luthers* in *Studien zu den Grundlagen der Reformation*, Vol. 5 (Giessen, 1967), pp. 225-237; Gerhard Ebeling, *Luther: An Introduction to His Thought* (Philadelphia, 1970), pp. 226-241; Ivar Asheim, ed., *The Church, Mysticism, Sanctification and the Natural* (Philadelphia, 1967), pp. 20-94; Walther von Loewenich, *Luther's Theology of the Cross* (Minneapolis, 1976), pp. 149-167. There are however scholars who hold that Luther did not break with mysticism so completely. E.g. Bengt R. Hoffman, *Luther and the Mystics* (Minneapolis, 1976), pp. 217-236; Rudolf Otto, *The Idea of the Holy*, 2nd ed. (New York, 1960), pp. 86-104.

18. *WA* 2, 111.4-5 (*LW* 42, 56).

19. *WA* 2, 112.37-113.3 (*LW* 42, 58).

20. *WA* 2, 88.1-15 (*LW* 42, 28).
21. *WA* 2, 88.13-15 (*LW* 42, 28).
22. *WA* 40/II, 329.27-330.17 (*LW* 12, 312).
23. *WA* 10/II, 377.12-13 (*LW* 43, 14).
24. *Bek*. 662 (*BC* 420).
25. *WA* 2, 85.9-12 (*LW* 42, 25).
26. *WA* 2, 85.2-4 (*LW* 42, 24).
27. *WA* 2, 115.33-35 (*LW* 42, 62).
28. *WA* 2, 127.38-128.2 (*LW* 42, 77).
29. *WA* 10/II, 389.11-15 (*LW* 43, 24-25).
30. *WA* 10/II, 396.10-13 (*LW* 43, 30).
31. *WA* 10/II, 407.4-7 (*LW* 43, 38).
32. *WA* 32, 413.33-34 (*LW* 21, 138).
33. *WA* 32, 414.24-25 (*LW* 21, 138).
34. *WA* 40/III, 503.21-22 (*LW* 13, 87-88).
35. *WA* 2, 127.3-5 (*LW* 42, 76).
36. *WA* 2, 83.5-7 (*LW* 42, 22).
37. *WA* 2, 127.28-31 (*LW* 42, 77).
38. *WA* 10/II, 376.3-5 (*LW* 43, 12).
39. *WA* 32, 417.6-7 (*LW* 21, 142); cf. *Bek*. 663 (*BC* 421).
40. *WA* 32, 418.19-21 (*LW* 21, 143); cf. *Bek*. 690 (*BC* 436).
41. *WA* 2, 81.29 (*LW* 42, 20).
42. *WA* 2, 127.34-40 (*LW* 42, 77).
43. *WA* 10/II, 395.14-17 (*LW* 43, 29).
44. *WA* 32, 401.26-28 (*LW* 21, 123).
45. *Bek*. 663 (*BC* 420-421).
46. *Ibid*.
47. *Bek*. 665 (*BC* 422).
48. *Bek*. 508 (*BC* 342).
49. *Bek*. 515 (*BC* 348).
50. *WA* 46, 81.34-82.2 (*LW* 24, 389).
51. *WA* 46, 89.17-21 (*LW* 24, 398).
52. Gustav Wingren, *Luther on Vocation* (Philadelphia, 1957), p. 185.
53. *WA* 43, 81.26-31 (*LW* 3, 288).
54. *WA* 43, 83.38-84.2 (*LW* 3, 291).
55. *WA* 43, 84.17-20 (*LW* 3, 292).

Chapter 2. The Invitation To Prayer

1. *WA* 2, 95.16-18 (*LW* 42, 37).
2. *WA* 2, 96.10-12 (*LW* 42, 38).
3. *WA* 2, 97.21-29 (*LW* 42, 39-40).
4. *WA* 2, 98.27-28 (*LW* 42, 41).

5. *WA* 2, 175.5-11 (*LW* 42, 87).
6. *WA* 2, 175.13-18 (*LW* 42, 87).
7. *WA* 2, 176.3-4 (*LW* 42, 88).
8. *WA* 32, 417.35-36 (*LW* 21, 143).
9. *WA* 45, 541.7-9 (*LW* 24, 88).
10. *WA* 46, 82.21-26, 37-83.3 (*LW* 24, 390).
11. *WA* 40/II, 329.19-20; 330.28-32 (*LW* 12, 312-313).
12. *WA* 40/II, 344.24-28; 345.17 (*LW* 12, 323).
13. *WA* 40/II, 345.20-26 (*LW* 12, 323).
14. *WA* 32, 493.9-13 (*LW* 21, 234).
15. Werner Elert, *The Christian Ethos* (Philadelphia, 1957), p. 133.
16. *WA* 18, 318.25-33; 320.28-32; 321.1-4 (*LW* 46, 34-35).
17. Wingren, *Luther on Vocation*, p. 113.
18. *WA* 51, 614.35-615.17 (*LW* 43, 235).
19. *WA* 51, 615.24-27; 616.20-21 (*LW* 43, 236).
20. *WA* 51, 604.19-30 (*LW* 43, 229-230).
21. *WA* 11, 273.31-274.6; 278.13-26 (*LW* 45, 119, 126).
22. Wingren, *Luther on Vocation*, p. 135.
23. *WA* 6, 242.22-25 (*LW* 44, 71).
24. *WA* 43, 82.36-38 (*LW* 3, 290).
25. *WA* 26, 504.30-31 (*LW* 37, 364).
26. *WA* 43, 512.15-26 (*LW* 5, 122).
27. *WA* 43, 513.4-8 (*LW* 5, 123).
28. *WA* 43, 513.9-15 (*LW* 5, 123) Translation altered.
29. *WA* 43, 513.29-33 (*LW* 5, 123-124).
30. *WA* 43, 514.5-19 (*LW* 5, 124).
31. *WA* 2, 87.9,14-15 (*LW* 42, 27).
32. *WA* 2, 94.18-22 (*LW* 42, 36).
33. *WA* 10/II, 398.7-8 (*LW* 43, 31).
34. *Bek.* 672 (*BC* 426).
35. *WA* 2, 176.5-20 (*LW* 42, 88).
36. *WATR* 5, 278, no. 5619.

Chapter 3. The Basis Of Prayer

1. *WA* 7, 571.5-7, 11-13, 16-18 (*LW* 21, 324-325).
2. *Bek.* 654 (*BC* 415).
3. *Bek.* 660 (*BC* 419).

4. *WA* 2, 98.23-28 (*LW* 42, 41).

5. *WA* 2, 99.14-16 (*LW* 42, 42).

6. *WA* 2, 111.27-33 (*LW* 42, 56).

7. *WA* 2, 112.14-15 (*LW* 42, 57).

8. *WA* 10/II, 391.21-24 (*LW* 43, 26).

9. *WA* 45, 540.21-25 (*LW* 24, 88).

10. *Bek.* 727 (*BC* 458).

11. *WA* 1, 233.10-11 (*LW* 31, 25).

12. *WA* 2, 93.35-37 (*LW* 42, 35).

13. *WA* 2, 105.36-106.2 (*LW* 42, 49).

14. *WA* 2, 107.10-13 (*LW* 42, 51).

15. *WA* 40/II 332.37; 333.13-17 (*LW* 12, 314).

16. *WA* 40/II, 333.22-27 (*LW* 12, 314-315).

17. *WA* 40/II, 333.32-34 (*LW* 12, 315).

18. *WA* 40/II, 336.22-23 (*LW* 12, 317).

19. *WA* 40/II, 337.19-21 (*LW* 12, 317).

20. Rudolf Damerau, *Luthers Gebetslehre 1515-1546* Zweiter Teil *Studien zu den Grundlagen der Reformation*, Vol. 14 (Marburg, 1977), pp. 170-171; Albrecht Peters, *Reformatorische Rechtfertigungsbotschaft zwischen tridentinischer und gegenwaertigem evangelischen Verstaendnis der Rechtfertigung* in *Luther-Jahrbuch 1964*, Franz Lau, ed. (Hamburg, 1964), pp. 96-102.

21. *WA* 56, 237.12-15 (*LW* 25, 222). *Lectures on Romans.* "For man cannot but seek his own advantage and love himself above all things. And this is the sum of all iniquities. Hence even in good things and virtues men seek themselves, that is, they seek to please themselves and applaud themselves." *WA* 56, 518.6 (*LW* 25, 513). "You are completely curved in upon yourself and pointed toward love of yourself. . . . "

22. *WA* 42, 122.12-13 (*LW* 1, 162).

23. *WA* 40/II, 385.26-27 (*LW* 12, 351).

24. *WA* 40/II, 380.33-36 (*LW* 12, 348).

25. *WA* 40/II, 386.25-28 (*LW* 12, 352).

26. *WA* 40/II, 391.29-36 (*LW* 12, 355-356).

27. *WA* 40/II, 393.36-394.17 (*LW* 12, 357).

28. *WA* 40/II, 395.33-36 (*LW* 12, 358).

29. *WA* 40/II, 434.32-435.21 (*LW* 12, 386).

30. *WA* 40/II, 438.19-22 (*LW* 12, 388).

31. *WA* 40/II, 446.21-23 (*LW* 12, 393).

32. *WA* 40/II, 449.17-20 (*LW* 12, 395).

33. *WA* 31/I, 134.34-135.18 (*LW* 14, 78).

34. *WA* 45, 541.10-13 (*LW* 24, 88).

35. *WA* 45, 542.14-26 (*LW* 24, 90).

36. *WA* 45, 542.32-543.6 (*LW* 24, 90).

37. *WA* 45, 701.39-40; 702.1-2, 8-14 (*LW* 24, 263-264).

38. *WA* 46, 84.34-41 (*LW* 24, 392-393).

39. *WA* 46, 85.23-24 (*LW* 24, 393).

40. *WA* 46, 88.36-89.12 (*LW* 24, 397).

Chapter 4. The Focus For Prayer

1. *Bek*. 415-416 (*BC* 292).

2. Rudolf Hermann, "Das Verhaeltnis von Rechtfertigung und Gebet" in *Gesammelte Studien zur Theologie Luthers und der Reformation* (Goettingen, 1960), pp. 11-43.

3. *WA* 44, 95.33-35 (*LW* 24, 405).

4. Karl Holl, "Was verstand Luther unter Religion?" in *Gesammelte Aufsaetze zur Kirchengeschichte* Vol. I *Luther* (Tuebingen, 1932), pp. 93-94.

5. *WA* 40/II, 357.35-358.23 (*LW* 12, 331).

6. *WA* 40/II, 407.30-34 (*LW* 12, 367).

7. *WA* 40/II, 407.39; 408.17-22 (*LW* 12, 367).

8. *WA* 40/II, 409.21-26 (*LW* 12, 368).

9. *WA* 40/II, 410/17-20 (*LW* 12, 368).

10. *WA* 40/II, 427.20-21; 428.18-20 (*LW* 12, 380-381).

11. *WA* 45, 541.24-27 (*LW* 24, 89).

12. *WA* 45, 546.36-547.6 (*LW* 24, 95).

13. *WA* 51, 625.19-24 (*LW* 43, 241).

14. *WA* 41, 212.38-213.30 (*LW* 13, 334). Cf. *LW* 24, 407 "But if we have this Mediator in our hearts and believe that He came from the Father, that He carried out the Father's command to take away sin and death from us, then we ourselves are able to pray. And such praying is acceptable to

God because of this Man, who mediated between the Father and us."

15. *WA* 2, 114.6-13 (*LW* 42, 59-60).
16. *WA* 2, 114.16-31 (*LW* 42, 60).
17. *WA* 6, 238.35; 239.4, 17-19 (*LW* 44, 66).
18. *WA* 38, 361.12-17 (*LW* 43, 196).
19. *WA* 38, 361.22-32 (*LW* 43, 196).
20. *WA* 38, 369 (*LW* 43, 204).
21. *Bek.* 514 (*BC* 347).
22. *Bek.* 679-680 (*BC* 430). *Large Catechism.* "Indeed the greatest need of all is to pray for our civil authorities and the government, for chiefly through them does God provide us our daily bread and all the comforts of this life. Although we have received from God all good things in abundance, we cannot

retain any of them or enjoy them in security and happiness unless he gives us a stable, peaceful government. For where dissension, strife, and war prevail, there our daily bread is taken away, or at least reduced."

23. *WA* 26, 33.32-33; 34.20-22, 27 (*LW* 28, 258-260).
24. *Bek.* 673-674 (*BC* 427).
25. *WA* 2, 86.5-6 (*LW* 42, 26).
26. See pp. 51 ff. above.
27. *WA* 2, 122.4-8 (*LW* 42, 70).
28. *WA* 38, 365.14-18 (*LW* 43, 200-201).
29. *Bek.* 511 (*BC* 345).
30. *Bek.* 650 (*BC* 413).
31. *WA* 30/II, 601.31-36 (*LW* 38, 105).
32. *WA* 30/II, 602.14-20 (*LW* 38, 106).
33. *WA* 2, 697.31-34 (*LW* 42, 115).

Chapter 5. The Efficacy Of Prayer

1. *WA* 2, 83.34-84.2 (*LW* 42, 23).
2. *WA* 10/II, 393.18-22 (*LW* 43, 28).
3. *WA* 32, 415.7-12 (*LW* 21, 139).
4. *WA* 40/II, 333.27-29 (*LW* 12, 315).
5. *WA* 40/II, 337.34-39 (*LW* 12, 318).
6. *WA* 40/II, 342.22-23 (*LW* 12, 321).
7. *WA* 40/II, 342.24-30 (*LW* 12, 321).
8. Werner Elert, *Der christliche Glaube* (Hamburg, 1960), pp. 145-146. Translation is mine.

9. *WA* 40/II, 356.19-23 (*LW* 12, 330).

10. *WA* 40/II, 417.22-25 (*LW* 12, 374).

11. *WA* 40/II, 417.33-35; 418.16-20 (*LW* 12, 374).

12. *WA* 40/II, 426.23-28, 35-36; 427.14-15 (*LW* 12, 380).

13. *WA* 40/II, 427.21-24 (*LW* 12, 380-381).

14. *WA* 40/II, 429.34-35 (*LW* 12, 383).

15. *WA* 40/II, 430.25-27 (*LW* 12, 383).

16. *WA* 40/II, 430.33-38; 431.17-25 (*LW* 12, 383-384).

17. *WA* 45, 541.27-47 (*LW* 24, 89).

18. *WA* 40/I, 585.23-31 (*LW* 26, 384).

19. *WA* 40/I, 586.20-22, 24-28 (*LW* 26, 385).

20. *WA* 38, 363.6-16 (*LW* 43, 198).

21. *WA* 38, 366.11-15 (*LW* 43, 201-202).

22. *WA* 44, 713.1 (*LW* 8, 183).

23. *Bek.* 459-460 (*BC* 315).

24. *Bek.* 654 (*BC* 415).

25. *Bek.* 655 (*BC* 416).

26. *Ibid.*

27. *WA* 12, 35.19-21, 24-25 (*LW* 53, 11).

28. *WA.* 12, 36.12-13 (*LW* 53, 12).

29. *WA.* 50, 641.20-21 (*LW* 41, 164).

30. *WA* 45, 681.25-28 (*LW* 24, 241).

31. *WA* 51, 482.25-28 (*LW* 41, 196).

32. *WA* 51, 485.1-7 (*LW* 41, 198).

33. *WA* 6, 238.10-22 (*WML* I, 233-234). Cf. *LW* 44, 65.

34. *WA* 6, 239.3-4 (*LW* 44, 66).

35. *WA* 6, 242.20-23 (*LW* 44, 71).

36. *WA* 47, 392.27.

37. *WA* 40/III, 506.18-19 (*LW* 13, 89).

38. *WA* 12, 36.12-13 (*LW* 53, 12).

39. *WATR* 3, 261, no. 3303.

40. *WA* 45, 540.19-21 (*LW* 24, 88).

41. *WA* 46, 87.10-12 (*LW* 24, 395).

42. *WA* 51, 599.30-31 (*LW* 43, 227).

43. *WA* 51, 603.30-34 (*LW* 43, 229).

44. *WA* 38, 375.1-2 (*LW* 43, 211).

45. *Bek.* 449 (*BC* 310).

46. *WA* 12, 47.5-10, 14-20 (*LW* 53, 101-102).

47. *WA* 12, 48.11-12 (*LW* 53, 103).

48. *WA* 12, 43.26-44.24 (*LW* 53, 97-98).

49. *WA* 6, 231.4-9 (*LW* 44, 56).

50. *WA* 30/III, 622.33-623.3
(*LW* 38, 133).

51. *WA* 30/III, 623 (*LW* 38,
133).

Chapter 6. The Purpose And Practice Of Prayer

1. *WA* 56, 375.3-5 (*LW* 25,
364-365).

2. *WA* 56, 375.18-19 (*LW* 25,
365).

3. *WA* 56, 376.2-6 (*LW* 25,
365).

4. *WA* 2, 124.27-29 (*LW* 42,
73).

5. *WA* 2, 125.18-126.3 (*LW*
42, 74-75).

6. *WA* 10/II, 400 (*LW* 43,
33).

7. *WA* 40/II, 355-356 (*LW*
12, 330).

8. *WA* 40/II, 452.33-34 (*LW*
12, 397).

9. *WA* 46, 84.21-23 (*LW* 24,
392).

10. *WA* 51, 606.21-25 (*LW* 43,
230-231).

11. *WA* 43, 82.22-31 (*LW* 3,
289).

12. *WATR* 5, 123, no. 5392
and 2, 262, no. 1912.

13. *Bek.* 678 (*BC* 429).

14. *WA* 56, 376.27-377.1
(*LCC* XV, 242).

15. *WA* 56, 378.12 (*LW* 25,
367).

16. *WA* 56, 380.20-21 (*LW* 25,
370).

17. *WA* 56, 380.33-36; 381.5-6
(*LW* 25, 370).

18. *WA* 2, 697.15-25 (*LW* 42,
114).

19. *WA* 31/I, 171.31-33 (*LW*
14, 96).

20. *WA* 40/II, 458-461 (*LW*
12, 403-405).

21. *WA* 40/II, 462.17-20 (*LW*
12, 405).

22. *WA* 40/II, 463-464 (*LW*
12, 407).

23. *WA* 2, 108.28-31 (*LW* 42,
53).

24. *Bek.* 672 (*BC* 426).

25. *WA* 2, 115.19-26 (*LW* 42,
61).

26. *Bek.* 674 (*BC* 427).

27. *WA* 32, 488.20-25 (*LW* 21,
228-229).

28. *WA* 43, 564.10-13 (*LW* 5,
197).

29. *WA* 43, 564.17-18 (*LW* 5,
197).

30. *WA* 32, 492.13-16 (*LW* 21,
233).

31. *WA* 40/II, 466.27-32 (*LW*
12, 407).

32. *WA* 31/I, 276.11-14.

33. *WA* 40/III, 18.21-25.

34. *WA* 10/III, 18.17-27 (*LW*
51, 77). Luther, speaking
of the apostle Paul's
preaching the Word of
God to his listeners at

the Areopagus in Athens, says: "When the Word took hold of their hearts, they forsook them [idols] of their own accord, and in consequence the thing fell of itself. Likewise, if I had seen them holding mass, I would have preached to them and admonished them. Had they heeded my admonition, I would have won them; if not, I would nevertheless not have torn them from it by the hair or employed any force, but simply allowed the Word to act and prayed for them. For the Word created heaven and earth and all things [Ps. 33:6]; the Word must do this thing, and not we poor sinners."

35. *WA* 40/III, 33.19-20.

36. *WA* 2, 146.8-9,12-14 (*LW* 31, 298).

37. *WA* 2, 147.19-23 (*LW* 31, 300).

38. *WA* 56, 260.23-261.2 (*LCC* XV, 114-115).

39. *Bek.* 659 (*BC* 418).

40. *WA* 10/II, 399.11-15 (*LW* 43, 32).

41. *WA* 2, 95.3-6, 8-10 (*LW* 42, 36-37).

42. *WA* 40/II, 422.28-35 (*LW* 12, 377-378).

43. *WA* 38, 359.11-17 (*LW* 43, 193-194).

44. *WA* 6, 234.31-33 (*LW* 44, 61).

45. *WA* 42, 659.6-7 (*LW* 3, 155).

46. *WA* 42, 659.9-10 (*LW* 3, 155).

47. *WA* 46, 76.2-6 (*LW* 24, 383).

48. *WA* 46, 77.22-23 (*LW* 24, 384).

49. *WA* 40/II, 427.30-34 (*LW* 12, 381).

50. *WA* 18, 528.6-8 (*LW* 14, 203).

51. *Bek.* 674 (*BC* 427).

52. *WA* 31/I, 126.29-34; 127.25-27 (*LW* 14, 74).

53. *WA* 32, 415.22-24 (*LW* 21, 140).

54. *WA* 32, 423.2-4, 5-8 (*LW* 21, 149).

55. *WA* 32, 488.35-37 (*LW* 21, 229).

56. *WA* 32, 490.15-17 (*LW* 21, 231).

57. *WA* 32, 491.32-34 (*LW* 21, 232).

58. *WA* 45, 539.37-39 (*LW* 24, 87).

59. *WA* 46, 81.18-19 (*LW* 24, 389).

60. *WA* 46, 81.20-24 (*LW* 24, 389).

61. *WATR* 4, 568, no. 4885.

62. Ingetraut Ludolphy,

"Luther als Beter", *Luther* 33 (1962): 130-131; cf. *CR* 3, 1060f.

63. *WATR* 5, 96-97, no. 5368.

64. *WA* 51, 618.23-24 (*LW* 43, 237).

65. *WA* 38, 360.37-361.3 (*LW* 43, 195).

66. *WA* 46, 92.7-10 (*LW* 24, 401).

67. *WA* 46, 92.26-27 (*LW* 24, 401).

68. *CR* 2, 159.

69. Martin Lehmann, *Justus Jonas Loyal Reformer* (Minneapolis, 1963), p. 66.

70. *WA* 32, 492.18-25 (*LW* 21, 233).

71. *WATR* 1, 442, no. 886.

Conclusion

1. Heiler, *Prayer*, p. 130.

2. *WA* 50, 658.29-659.4 (*LW* 34, 285).

3. *WA* 50, 659.6-7 (*LW* 34, 285).

4. *WA* 50, 659.10-13 (*LW* 34, 285-286).

5. *WA* 50, 659.30-35 (*LW* 34, 286).

6. *WA* 50, 660.2-4 (*LW* 34, 287).

7. Damerau, *Luthers Gebetslehre 1515-1546*, 14, pp. 26-28.

8. *WA* 31/I, 95.36; 96.19-34 (*LW* 14, 60-61).

9. *WA* 31/I, 96.35; 97.18-19 (*LW* 14, 61).

10. See page 75 above.

11. The expression "theocentric" was employed especially by Gustav Aulén and Anders Nygren of Sweden as a key to a proper understanding of Luther's theology. See Gustav Aulén, *The Faith of the Christian Church* (Philadelphia, 1948), pp. 60-65, and Anders Nygren, *Agape and Eros* (Philadelphia, 1953), pp. 681-691. See also Philip Watson, *Let God be God An Interpretation of the Theology of Martin Luther* (Philadelphia, 1949), pp. 33-38.

12. *WA* 46, 83.13-14 (*LW* 24, 391).

13. *WATR* 1, 183, no. 421.

14. *WA* 10/I/2, 183.27-28.

15. *WA* 25, 390.18-27.

16. *WA* 32, 420.9-10 (*LW* 21, 146).

17. *WA* 32, 422.16-18 (*LW* 21, 148).

18. *WA* 40/III, 26.32-37; 27.13-14.

19. *WATR* 2, 628, no. 2742a.

20. *WA* 25, 390.18-26.

21. *WA* 38, 364.17-27 (*LW* 43, 200).

22. *WA* 46, 81.18-24 (*LW* 24, 389).

23. *WA* 43, 678.5-7 (*LW* 5, 361).

24. *WABr* 9, 89.12-16.

25. *WA* 43, 82.15-17, 22-24 (*LW* 3, 289).

26. *WA* 7, 28.13-17 (*LW* 31, 355). The translation of this sentence in *Luther's Works* is not entirely accurate here. I have translated it from the German version in *WA*.

27. *WA* 43, 381.16-18 (*LW* 4, 340).

28. See pp. 130-131 above.

29. *WATR* 6, 162-163, no. 6751.

30. *WATR* 2, 629, no. 2742b.

31. *WA* 49, 588.15-18 (*LW* 51, 333).

32. *WA* 7, 32.5-11 (*LW* 31, 362).

33. *WA* 3, 340.13-14.

34. *WA* 38, 221.32-35 (*LW* 38, 177-178).

35. *WA* 2, 82.29-32 (*LW* 42, 21).

36. *WA* 30/III, 170.29-35 (*LW* 38, 88-89).

37. *WA* 42, 321.33-34 (*LW* 2, 84).

38. *WA* 35, 468.1-4 (*LW* 53, 305).

39. Gunnar Wertelius, *Oratio continua Das Verhaeltnis zwischen Glaube und Gebet in der Theologie Luthers* (Lund, 1970), p. 217. This volume presents a thorough and well-documented study of prayer in Luther's theology. Translation is mine.

40. *WA* 28, 182.21-27.

41. *WA* 44, 574.35-575.1 (*LW* 7, 369) Translation slightly altered.

BIBLIOGRAPHY

Althaus, Paul. *Die Theologie Martin Luthers*. Guetersloh, 1962.

Asheim, Ivar, ed. *The Church, Mysticism, Sanctification and the Natural*. Philadelphia, 1967.

Aulén, Gustav. *The Faith of the Christian Church*. Translated by Eric H. Wahlstrom and G. Everett Arden. Philadelphia, 1948.

Beintker, Horst. "Zu Luthers Verstaendnis vom geistlichen Leben des Christen im Gebet." *Luther-Jahrbuch 31* (1964):47-68.

Bornkamm, Heinrich. *Luther's World of Thought*. Translated by Martin H. Bertram. St. Louis, 1958.

Brokering, Herbert F. *Luther's Prayers*. Minneapolis, 1967.

Carlson, Edgar M. *The Reinterpretation of Luther*. Philadelphia, 1948.

Damerau, Rudolf. *Die Demut in der Theologie Luthers. Studien zu den Grundlagen der Reformation*. Vol. 5. Giessen, 1967.

_____. *Luthers Gebetslehre bis 1515*. Part 1. *Studien zu den Grundlagen der Reformation*. Vol. 12. Marburg 1975.

_____. *Luthers Gebetslehre 1515-1546*. Part 2. *Studien zu den Grundlagen der Reformation*. Vol. 14. Marburg, 1977.

Ebeling, Gerhard. *Luther: An Introduction to His Thought*. Philadelphia, 1970.

Elert, Werner. *The Christian Ethos*. Translated by Carl J. Schindler. Philadelphia, 1957.

_____. *Der christliche Glaube*. Hamburg, 1960.

Heiler, Friedrich. *Das Gebert Eine religionsgeschichtliche und religionspsychologische Untersuchung.* 5th ed. Muenchen, 1923.

_____ . *Prayer A Study in the History and Psychology of Religion.* Translated by Samuel McComb. New York, 1932.

Hermann, Rudolf. "Das Verhaeltnis von Rechtfertigung und Gebet" *Gesammelte Studien zur Theologie Luthers und der Reformation.* Goettingen, 1960, pp. 11-43

_____ . *Luthers Theologie. Gesammelte und nachgelassene Werke I.* Goettingen, 1967.

Hoffman, Bengt R. *Luther and the Mystics.* Minneapolis, 1976.

Holl, Karl. "Was verstand Luther unter Religion?" (1917). *Gesammelte Aufsaetze zur Kirchengeschichte.* Vol. I: *Luther.* 6th ed. Tuebingen, 1932, pp. 1-110.

Koestlin, Julius. *Luthers Theologie in ihrer geschichtlichen Entwicklung und ihrem inneren Zusammenhang.* 2 vols. 2nd ed. Stuttgart, 1901.

Koestlin, Julius, and Kawerau, Gustav. *Martin Luther: Sein Leben und seine Schriften.* 2 vols. 5th ed. Berlin, 1903.

Kooiman, Willem Jan. *Luther and the Bible.* Translated by John Schmidt. Philadelphia, 1961.

Lehmann, Martin. *Justus Jonas Loyal Reformer.* Minneapolis, 1963.

Loewenich, Walther von. *Luther's Theology of the Cross.* Minneapolis, 1976.

Ludolphy, Ingetraut. "Luther als Beter." *Luther* 33 (1962): 128-144.

Nygren, Anders. *Agape and Eros.* Translated by Philip S. Watson. Philadelphia, 1953.

Otto, Rudolf. *The Idea of the Holy.* 2nd ed. New York, 1960.

Peters, Albrecht. "Reformatorische Rechtfertigungsbotschaft zwischen tridentinischer und gegenwaertigem evangelischen Verstaendnis der Rechtfertigung." *Luther-Jahrbuch* 31 (1964): 77-128.

Scheel, Otto. *Martin Luther: Vom Katholizismus zur Reformation.* 2 vols. Tuebingen, 1916, 1917.

_____ . "Taulers Mystik und Luthers reformatorische Entdeckung." *Festgabe fuer D. Dr. Julius Kaftan.* Tuebingen, 1920, pp. 298-318.

Schmidt, Kurt Dietrich. "Luther lehrt beten." *Luther* 34 (1963): 31-41.

Schulz, Frieder. *Die Gebete Luthers Quellen und Forschungen zur Reformationsgeschichte.* Vol. 44. Guetersloh, 1976.

Vajta, Vilmos. *Luther on Worship.* Translated by U. S. Leupold. Philadelphia, 1958.

Watson, Philip. *Let God be God An Interpretation of the Theology of Martin Luther.* Philadelphia, 1949.

Wertelius, Gunnar. *Oratio continua Das Verhaeltnis von Glaube und Gebet in der Theologie Martin Luthers Studia Theologica Lundensia* 32. Lund, 1970.

Wingren, Gustav. *Luther on Vocation.* Philadelphia, 1957.

INDEX OF SUBJECTS

INDEX OF PERSONS

INDEX TO SCRIPTURE PASSAGES